SOUP CLUB

80 Cozy Recipes for Creative, Plant-Based Soups and Stews to Share

CAROLINE WRIGHT

Illustrations by WILLOW HEATH

Andrews McMeel
PUBLISHING®

To my boys—Garth, Henry, and Theodore—for
being at the heart of every community, table, or life
I could ever hope to celebrate. You are my joy.

Andrews McMeel Publishing
a division of Andrews McMeel Universal
1130 Walnut Street, Kansas City, Missouri 64106

www.andrewsmcmeel.com
www.soupclubcookbook.com

FSC
www.fsc.org
MIX
Paper from
responsible sources
FSC® C109093

21 22 23 24 25 SHO 10 9 8 7 6 5 4 3 2 1
ISBN: 978-1-5248-6892-5
Library of Congress Control Number: 2021936508

Editor: Jean Z. Lucas
Designer: Amy Chinn
Art Director: Diane Marsh
Photographer: Joshua Huston
Production Manager: Carol Coe
Production Editor: Dave Shaw

ATTENTION: SCHOOLS AND BUSINESSES
Andrews McMeel books are available at quantity discounts with
bulk purchase for educational, business, or sales promotional use.
For information, please e-mail the Andrews McMeel Publishing
Special Sales Department: specialsales@amuniversal.com.

Contents

The Soup Club Story

At the base of every bowl of soup is a story, often rooted in profound resourcefulness, creativity, and rich personal history. The soups in this book are no exception.

It was mid-February in Seattle when I found out I had a tumor in my brain. After learning that it was cancerous and being told I had a year to live, I noticed the gray and rain differently than I ever had before in the year since moving there; it made me cold, colder still with a shaved head studded with staples clinging to tender wounds. Cooking was out of the question—too physical—which stole from me my belonging and purpose in my own home. It was as if I had already started to disappear. I spent those days shuffling to the kitchen in my slippers, taking note of the intentional movements demonstrated by the occupational therapist I met with after my brain surgery as I moved, to rummage the refrigerator for leftover takeout. Eating soulless food made by strangers behind a counter made me feel empty, I noticed, as I pawed the contents of the containers in my refrigerator for some sign of life with my spoon. The lifeless food I was eating had made me feel lifeless, too.

I was writing a journal online at that point, one where I was documenting my thoughts and feelings for my sons in case my prognosis proved to be accurate; it was frequented by everyone I'd ever met and many I hadn't. There I sounded a call for a kind of help that I felt I desperately needed: one for homemade soup. I needed soulful food, meals that would help me and my family heal. One of my dearest and oldest friends managed the flood of responses, a rushing tide of Mason jars with my name on them. Suddenly I was eating soup every day.

Soup began to take on a kind of electricity in my mind, a current that connected me to my community and conveyed their flow of support and sorrow and hope in a digestible way. Other than my keyboard, my simmering saucepan was the only conduit that tethered me to the outside world. Friends and strangers brought me soup, quietly placed in a cooler by our front door. Soup became a kind of currency of support transmitted through this magician's box; into it went soup, from it came hope. Eventually, this soup—mostly lentil, the overwhelmingly popular choice in my area of Seattle in which to infuse words that cannot be spoken—filled in the broken parts of my exhausted, worried being. Just like that I was full. And restored, ready to cook.

Every part of my life had shifted since my diagnosis, filled with a kind of meaning that perhaps only those negotiating mortality can fully comprehend. I had an acute clarity and profound appreciation for simplicity. In the process of finding strength, I listened to my body's call for gentle foods and researched a point of entry for what my health could look like. My decisions were brutal, sudden, and unyielding—overnight I severed lifelong romances with favorite ingredients, meals, and recipes and with them, any hopes I'd held for my beloved career as a cookbook author. I no longer ate sugar, chocolate, or gluten, along with what otherwise read like a grocery list of produce, in an effort to calm my system as I sent it into war.

At first, I baked. I quested after these pillars of celebration and comfort as if following a road map to the person I was becoming, required for what I recognized as a joyful life shared with friends and family. It was also a way to translate the meaning of my past—my beloved baking recipes, the result of my most favorite projects—using my new vocabulary. It was challenging and rewarding and made me feel like myself.

The Rebirthday

Before I knew it, I had baked my way to a year from my diagnosis, the day I was told I was unlikely to see. In my kitchen was a cake I'd figured out along the way that I used to celebrate my rebirthday. Creating the recipe over numerous trials, tweaking the ingredients in a way that suggested, even if only in that single case, a kind of mastery of this unknown palette to result in a celebration of life, community, and family, made me feel whole, powerful—healthy, even.

Being diagnosed with an "impossible" cancer at a young age is surreal to say the least. The thing that no one says out loud, however, is that surviving it after emptying out the pockets of your life is surreal, too. Both are hard and strange. You survive to live a life you don't recognize, surrounded by a lot of people who might always see you as sick or less capable somehow. I was confused, scared, and searching for answers—the only thing I knew for sure is that I wasn't done cooking or telling stories.

That is when I started to make soup and bring it to people I love, drop it on friends' porches with some chocolate chip cookies during the rainiest months of Seattle winter. I was determined to return the loan of comfort I was given in spades and knew that cooking and connecting with people from an authentic place of love would lead me back to a version of myself that I recognize. Having people other than my family have a visceral reaction to my food restored my confidence as a cook. Nourishing them also nourished me.

There is something magical about soup, I discovered, as I cooked vats of the stuff each week. You assemble these disparate ingredients, and with time and care, they transform into something cohesive and altogether different. As with baked goods, soup makes the person it is served to feel something. The biggest characteristic difference between them, however, is utility and intent: Baked goods are usually celebratory; soup is somewhat its opposite. Soup holds a humble kind of magic. Foremost among its most impressive displays of sleight of hand, it transformed the gray and rain of Seattle winter into, simply, "soup weather" and me into a "survivor."

These are the recipes from my soup club, this quirky community of soup-obsessed loved ones in my corner of Seattle who let me feed the people they love most. The recipes in this book are expressions of resilience and hope and hold in them deep gratitude for health and life itself. Writing this book, bringing these recipes to other families, has been a passion project of incredible proportion with, as it turns out, commiserate reward. It is truly an honor and measure of great fortune that this book is in your hands. Thank you for being a part of my story. I sincerely hope you enjoy every spoonful.

Soup Lady Wisdom

All of the recipes in this book come from a soup club run by me, Caroline Wright, in Seattle, where the weather demands soup most of the year. Making many quarts of soup each week provided a helpful playground for me to learn a lot about soup making and build on the ideas I already held as a professional cook. Before we dig into the recipes, I thought I'd share a few tips I learned along the way. Let's step into the kitchen together.

The difference between good and great soup—

Soup is so simple that the details really matter. These recipes do not call for stock, homemade or otherwise, because who wants to make what is essentially a pot of soup before making another pot of soup, anyway? So the timing, amount of water, and seasoning become especially important for a complex—meaning, truly delicious and surprising—bowl of soup. That's the reason I include salt measurements in the recipes, so you have a general idea of what I think it takes to make these soups taste amazing. This is also why you'll notice that most of the soups are finished with lemon or some kind of vinegar; the acid helps to balance the flavors in the brew. Each recipe also has a specific water measurement, too, that's added only at the beginning; water is a vehicle to build flavor that has to be developed. If adjusted, as in adding water at the end of cooking to thin or stretch the yield, you'll be diluting the flavor that was developed over its cooking time. That said, thickness is another detail that is super important in leveling up your soup game (ensure that soup stays in the "soup" realm rather than one of "baby food"), so if you do

need to thin it out a little, re-season with salt and acid.

While we're talking about water—

Tap water is assumed for these recipes, though discouraged if your local tap water has a strong odor or flavor. If you don't prefer to drink your tap water, don't use it in soup, either; instead, opt for a cheap jug of the filtered stuff at the store.

Other things you might need from the store—

The stovetop versions of these recipes were written for a cast-iron (enameled preferred) 3 to 5-quart Dutch oven, which I believe to be a requirement for any hopeful soup cook. It's superior for its heat retention, reliability, and versatility for either stovetop or oven use. If you don't have one, a small stockpot works, too. In terms of ingredients, you may notice a few ingredients that are new to you, like nutritional yeast (a staple for plant-based cooking as far as I'm concerned—it's widely available at grocery stores, including Trader Joe's). The recipes for ones that you can make, like garam masala, or any of the seasoning blends I use, are included in the back of the book, starting on page 162.

A note about the Instant Pot and some other recipe musings—

All of these recipes were developed for the stovetop, as burbling pots steaming up my kitchen ranks high on my life goals since living in Seattle. Despite being a traditionalist and general Luddite, I concede that the Instant Pot is a helpful tool for making soup—so I adapted every recipe in this book to suit it, which you can check out starting on page 134. All the recipes in this book were developed and tested with the Instant Pot DUO60 6 Qt 7-in-1 Multi-Use. I love not having to soak beans overnight in order to make soup, a real game-changer for me. The hiss of the valve release became a regular addition to the din of my kitchen. (By the way, I wrote these recipes to leave the release method open to the preference and comfort level of the cook by deferring to the helpful guidelines in the Instant Pot manual.) I'll never be convinced that it results in a better soup than the old-fashioned way, however, which is why I consider the Instant Pot recipes to be variations (indicated by the handy little icon in the upper right-hand corner of the recipe page). If you are looking for a hands-off way to make soup without a gadget, I recommend transferring the pot to a preheated 350°F oven for the duration of its lengthy simmer (often about an hour).

Two recipe versions, each tested at least twice by interns and family. ... I swam in soup for two years while making this book. Here are my tips on freezing and storage—

The best way to freeze soup is to transfer it to your preferred containers (plastic, glass, or even freezer bags) after it has fully cooled, leaving about ½ inch of room at the top because ... science (to allow room for it to expand). To thaw frozen soup, stick it in the refrigerator for 1 to 2 days before reheating. If you have an Instant Pot, this process can be made instant also: Release the soup from its container by running it under hot water and place it in

the metal insert, then follow directions in the recipes starting on page 134 to close lid, set to PRESSURE COOK (HIGH setting), and cook the soup brick for 15 minutes. This isn't to say I haven't run a container under hot water to release the soup iceberg from its confines, slopped it into a saucepan with a bit of water, and crossed my fingers that I don't burn or overcook it as it melts into a very last-minute dinner. I don't recommend it.

On the subject of recommendations—

I have written recipes for a long time, and something I've learned is that there are so many variables—innumerable, really—between what I write down and what ends up on a reader's plate. It's a dance that involves differences in factors ranging from equipment, heat source, altitude, and so many others in between. Where it lands is judgment, which is the job of a cook to make it theirs. Including too much detail makes even the simplest recipes daunting, which is entirely against my being as a cook and friend in the kitchen. When I teach classes, I encourage the cooks I'm chatting with to sense their food fully: listen to it, smell it, taste it. Use the recipe as a guideline. I've written these recipes that way, with measurements for salt in parentheses and timing as a ballpark suggestion following how the ingredients should look, feel, or sound, with the focus to be intended on the descriptor. The only exception to this call for empowerment is the measurements for the size of vegetable cuts—you'll notice there are recipes that have 3-inch potato pieces in them, which may feel insane. Trust me, digging a spoon into a warm potato at the bottom of the bowl is part of the charm of these recipes ... and these recipes work as written, you have my word.

All About Beans

I love working with beans: They're a cheap and healthy form of plant-based protein. The recipes in this book exclusively use the dried variety. All you really need to know before using dried beans in a recipe (either traditional or Instant Pot) is to sort through them. It seems fussy, I know, but let's be real: No one likes biting into gravel. I simply transfer the amount of beans used in a recipe to a colander, sift through with my fingers and pluck out cracked or discolored ones, as well as any rogue pebbles, then either transfer them to a bowl to be covered with water and left on my counter overnight, or dumped directly into a recipe for the Instant Pot. For those that soak overnight, I prefer to strain off the soaking water and start with fresh water for cooking, though I'm aware that there are cooks who swear by doing the opposite. This isn't the only facet of cooking beans that incites debate among food nerds, actually, from if and when to salt their water to whether or not tomatoes make beans tough. My research of all the variables required to achieve a properly cooked bean landed me facing two truths: Beans can be tough due to their age and care during storage, and synchronizing the addition of flavor ingredients (salt/tomatoes) won't change that. The solution for a tender bean is simple: Cook it until it no longer tastes tough to you. Last thing before you race to the store:

2 cups dried beans = 1 pound

Oh, and there is a bean glossary on page 166 for substitutions and sweet paintings of beans, you bean nerd, you. And that, officially, is all I have to say about beans.

Ribollita

Ribollita

To level up your soup bowl, drizzle this with olive oil, sprinkle it with grated Parmesan, or scatter it with pepper flakes. Serve over a slice of crusty bread in the name of tradition.

Makes about 8 bowlfuls (or 3 quarts)

¼ cup olive oil
1 medium onion, chopped
2 celery stalks, chopped
1 medium carrot, peeled and chopped
Kosher salt and freshly ground black pepper
2 medium potatoes, sweet or regular, peeled and cut into
   2-inch chunks
1 small bunch broccoli rabe, cut into 1-inch pieces
1 small bunch kale, ribs and stems removed, thinly sliced
1 cup dried Great Northern beans, soaked overnight
4 sprigs thyme
1 (14.5-ounce) can diced tomatoes
1 teaspoon freshly squeezed lemon juice, plus more to
   taste

1 / Heat oil in a large, heavy pot over medium heat until hot. Add onion, celery, and carrot; season generously with salt and pepper (about 1 teaspoon salt and ½ teaspoon pepper). Cook, stirring often, until vegetables have softened, about 10 minutes. Stir in potatoes, broccoli rabe, kale, beans, thyme, tomatoes, and 8 cups (2 quarts) water; season very generously with salt (about 2 teaspoons). Cover and bring to a boil.

2 / Lower heat to slowly simmer soup, covered and without stirring, until beans are tender, about 1½ hours. Stir in lemon juice. Season soup with additional salt and lemon juice to taste. Remove thyme sprigs before serving.

fading into red
green leaves in my soup
harvest moon

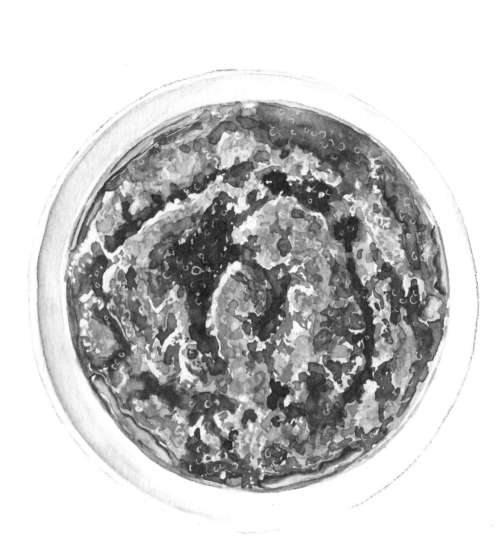

Tomato and Quinoa Soup

Tomato and Quinoa Soup

Drizzle this soup with olive oil or stir in a tender green, such as arugula or baby spinach, like a good vegan. It also wouldn't be a bad moment to wake up next to a grilled cheese sandwich, either, just sayin'.

Makes about 12 bowlfuls (or 3 quarts)

1 medium onion, cut into 8 wedges with root end intact
4 cloves garlic, peeled
4 large carrots (1 pound), peeled and cut into 1-inch pieces
1 teaspoon thyme leaves (4 sprigs, stripped)
¼ cup olive oil, divided
Kosher salt and freshly ground black pepper
2 tablespoons tomato paste
2 bay leaves, fresh or dried
1 (28-ounce) can diced tomatoes
1 (28-ounce) can crushed tomatoes
1 cup uncooked quinoa, rinsed if desired
3 tablespoons agave nectar
1 teaspoon cider vinegar

1 / Heat broiler with rack about 5 inches away from heat. On a large rimmed baking sheet, toss onion, garlic, carrots, and thyme with 2 tablespoons oil; season generously with pinches of salt and pepper. Broil, tossing occasionally, until vegetables are golden brown in spots and tender when pierced, about 10 minutes. Transfer vegetables to a blender jar with 1 cup water; blend, cracking lid and covering with a towel to release steam, until smooth. Season purée with salt and pepper (about 1 teaspoon salt and ½ teaspoon pepper). Place blender jar near stove.

2 / In a large, heavy pot, heat remaining oil over medium heat until hot. Carefully stir in tomato paste (it will spatter); cook, stirring, until the oil turns red and the paste is broken apart (about 3 minutes). Stir in vegetable purée, scraping bottom and sides of pot with wooden spoon to release any caramelized tomato. Stir in bay leaves, tomatoes (both diced and crushed), quinoa, and 4 cups (1 quart) water. Simmer soup, uncovered and stirring occasionally, until thickened, flavors have blended, and quinoa is cooked, about 30 minutes. Stir in agave and vinegar. Season soup to taste with additional salt, pepper, agave, and vinegar to taste. Remove bay leaves before serving.

lunch thermos
carrying the warmth of home
back to school

Pumpkin-Coconut Soup with Curry Leaves

Pumpkin-Coconut Soup with Curry Leaves

Stir in rotisserie chicken or raw cashews (soaked overnight) to add more protein like the cool kid you are.

Makes about 8 bowlfuls (or 4 quarts)

6 cloves garlic, peeled
1 (1-inch) piece fresh ginger, peeled and sliced
1 large onion, peeled and quartered
¼ cup coconut oil
¼ cup firmly packed curry leaves, fresh or dried
2 tablespoons Homemade Curry Powder (page 162) or
    store-bought
1 (15-ounce) can pure pumpkin purée
Kosher salt
1 small kabocha squash (about 2 pounds), peeled, seeds removed,
    and cut into very large (3-inch) chunks
4 cups cubed, peeled butternut squash (from 1 small)
2 small sweet potatoes or yams, peeled and cut into 2-inch pieces
2 cups full-fat coconut cream (from a well-shaken carton, such as
    Aroy-D brand; sold in Asian markets)
1 teaspoon Homemade Garam Masala (page 162) or store-bought
2 tablespoons freshly squeezed lemon juice, plus more to taste
Pumpkin seeds for serving, optional

1 / In a blender jar, combine garlic, ginger, onion, and ¼ cup water; blend until smooth. Place blender jar next to stove.

2 / Heat oil in a large, heavy pot over high heat until hot. Add curry leaves (they will spit and snap in the hot oil) and cook until they begin to brown, about 1 minute. Stir in curry powder, pumpkin purée, reserved blended onion mixture, and 6 cups (1½ quarts) water; season very generously with salt (about 2 teaspoons). Cover and bring to a boil.

3 / Add kabocha and butternut squash and sweet potatoes. Lower heat to slowly simmer soup, uncovered and without stirring, until kabocha is tender when pierced with a knife and liquid has reduced to below the height of the squash by about ½ inch, about 1 hour. Stir in coconut cream and garam masala, gently breaking apart potatoes. Raise heat to quickly simmer soup until broth coats the back of a spoon, about 10 minutes. Stir in lemon juice. Season soup with additional salt and lemon juice to taste. Serve soup topped with pumpkin seeds, if desired.

*biting the curry leaf
the jack-o'-lantern's
toothless grin*

Egyptian Chickpea and Okra Stew

Egyptian Chickpea and Okra Stew

If you have carnivores at your table, sauté a bit of ground lamb and spoon it over the top of the stew before serving.

Makes about 8 bowlfuls (or 3 quarts)

½ cup olive oil
1 large onion, chopped
3 large celery stalks, chopped
Kosher salt
2 cloves garlic, chopped
¼ cup nutritional yeast
1 tablespoon ground cumin
2 teaspoons ground coriander
1 pound dried chickpeas, soaked overnight
1 pound fresh or frozen okra, cut into 1-inch pieces
1 (28-ounce) can crushed tomatoes
1 dried Árbol chile, optional
2 tablespoons freshly squeezed lemon juice, plus more
   to taste

1 / Heat oil in a large, heavy pot over medium heat until hot. Add onion and celery; season with salt (about ½ teaspoon). Cook, stirring often, until vegetables have softened, about 10 minutes.

2 / Stir in garlic, yeast, cumin, coriander, chickpeas, okra, tomatoes, chile (if using), and 8 cups (2 quarts) water; season very generously with salt (about 1 tablespoon). Cover and bring to a boil.

3 / Lower heat to slowly simmer stew, uncovered and stirring occasionally, until chickpeas are just cooked through but firm, about 1 hour. Raise heat to quickly simmer stew, stirring occasionally to break apart the okra, until chickpeas are soft and broth has reduced to a thick, flavorful gravy, about 1 hour. Stir in lemon juice. Season stew with salt and additional lemon juice to taste. Discard chile, if used, before serving.

first frost
the soup container
thaws

Teddy's Black Bean Soup

Teddy's Black Bean Soup

Eat this as soup or serve it over rice, topped with any and all manner of your favorite tasty things hiding in the drawers and doors of your refrigerator. You can't do it wrong.

Makes about 6 bowlfuls (or 1½ quarts)

1 cup olive oil
1 large onion, chopped
1 large green bell pepper, chopped
Kosher salt
6 cloves garlic, finely chopped
1 tablespoon ground cumin
1 tablespoon dried oregano
2 tablespoons cider vinegar, plus more to taste
1 pound dried black beans, soaked overnight

1 / Heat oil in a large, heavy pot over medium heat until hot. Add onion and bell pepper; season generously with salt (about 1 teaspoon). Cook slowly, stirring often, until vegetables have softened, about 10 minutes. Stir in garlic, cumin, oregano, vinegar, beans, and 8 cups (2 quarts) water. Season very generously with salt (about 2 teaspoons). Cover and bring to a boil.

2 / Lower heat to slowly simmer soup, uncovered and stirring occasionally, until beans are just cooked through but firm, about 1 hour. Raise heat to quickly simmer soup, uncovered and stirring occasionally, until beans just begin to break apart and broth has reduced to a thick, flavorful gravy, about 1 hour. Season soup with additional salt and vinegar to taste.

trusted recipe
the taste
of friendship

Moroccan Vegetable Stew

Moroccan Vegetable Stew

To make this chunky stew even cozier, serve it over steamed couscous or millet.

Makes about 8 bowlfuls (or 3 quarts)

1 small bunch cilantro (about 10 sprigs)
1 small bunch parsley (about 10 sprigs)
¼ cup firmly packed mint leaves (stripped from about 4 sprigs), finely chopped
½ cup olive oil
1 large onion, chopped
2 cloves garlic, chopped
1 (1-inch) piece fresh ginger, peeled and chopped
Kosher salt
½ cup Homemade Harissa (page 163) or 2 tablespoons store-bought
2 teaspoons ground cumin
1 teaspoon dried turmeric
2 strips orange zest, peeled with a vegetable peeler and thinly sliced
1 (28-ounce) can diced tomatoes
1 cup dried chickpeas, soaked overnight
1 large sweet potato, peeled and quartered
3 large carrots, peeled and cut into 2-inch chunks
½ medium head cauliflower, cored and cut into bite-sized florets (about 3 cups)
2 medium zucchini, quartered lengthwise and sliced into ¾-inch chunks
1 tablespoon freshly squeezed lemon juice, plus more to taste

1 / Separate cilantro leaves from stems; finely chop both separately. Repeat with parsley; place herb stems in one bowl and leaves in another, combining cilantro, parsley, and mint. (You should have 1 firmly packed tablespoon combined stems and ½ firmly packed cup combined leaves; set aside.)

2 / Heat oil in a large, heavy pot over medium heat until hot. Add onion, garlic, and ginger; season generously with salt (about 1 teaspoon). Lower heat and cook slowly, stirring often, until onion is shiny, clear, and tender, about 15 minutes. Stir in harissa, cumin, turmeric, zest, reserved herb stems, tomatoes, chickpeas, potato, carrots, and 6 cups (1½ quarts) water; season very generously with salt (about 2 teaspoons). Cover and bring to a boil.

3 / Lower heat to slowly simmer stew, uncovered and stirring occasionally, until chickpeas are just cooked through but firm, about 1 hour. Add cauliflower and zucchini. Raise heat to quickly simmer stew, stirring occasionally, until vegetables are tender but still crisp, about 5 minutes. Stir in lemon juice and reserved chopped herb leaves. Season stew with additional salt and lemon juice to taste.

lifting fog
the warm scent
of stew

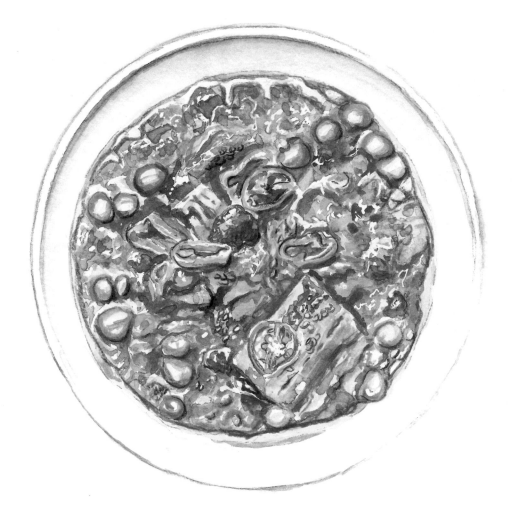

Parsi Squash Stew

Parsi Squash Stew

Once it's in your bowl, turn up the spice as high as you can take it by adding a sloppy spoonful of sambal oelek.

Makes about 8 bowlfuls (or 3 quarts)

¼ cup coconut oil
1 large onion, chopped
Kosher salt
1 (1-inch) piece fresh ginger, peeled and chopped
4 cloves garlic, finely chopped
1½ teaspoons ground turmeric
1 teaspoon ground coriander
1 teaspoon ground cumin
¼ teaspoon ground cloves
2 bay leaves, fresh or dried
1 (14.5-ounce) can diced tomatoes
½ cup dried chickpeas, soaked overnight
½ cup dried mung beans
½ cup dried red lentils
1 large delicata squash (about 1 pound), halved lengthwise, seeds scooped away and composted, and cut into 2-inch pieces (do not peel)
4 cups baby spinach (¾ of a 5-ounce container)
2 teaspoons cider vinegar, plus more to taste

1 / Heat oil in a large, heavy pot over medium heat until hot. Add onion; season generously with salt (about 1 teaspoon). Reduce heat and cook slowly until onion is shiny, clear, and tender, about 15 minutes. Stir in ginger, garlic, turmeric, coriander, cumin, cloves, bay leaves, tomatoes, chickpeas, beans, lentils, squash, and 8 cups (2 quarts) water; season very generously with salt (about 2 teaspoons). Cover and bring to a boil.

2 / Lower heat to slowly simmer stew, uncovered and without stirring, until chickpeas are just cooked through but firm, about 1 hour. Gently stir in spinach by the handful, taking care not to break apart squash. Stir in vinegar. Season stew with additional salt and vinegar to taste. Remove bay leaves before serving.

soup steam
evaporating
all my worries

White Bean Chili with Tomatillo

White Bean Chili with Tomatillo

Top this soup with avocado. To please your carnivorous friends (or switch up leftovers), brown some ground chicken and add the soup over top to reheat. But let's be real: If you top it with avocado in the first place, there won't be any leftovers.

Makes about 8 bowlfuls (or 2 quarts)

¼ cup avocado oil
1 large onion, chopped
1 large green bell pepper, chopped
Kosher salt
6 cloves garlic, chopped
2 tablespoons Green Chili Powder (page 163)
1½ pounds tomatillos (about 12), husk removed and roughly chopped
1 pound dried Great Northern beans, soaked overnight
2 tablespoons firmly packed chopped cilantro leaves

1 / Heat oil in a large, heavy pot over medium heat until hot. Add onion and bell pepper; season generously with salt (about 1 teaspoon). Cook slowly, stirring often, until vegetables have softened, about 10 minutes. Stir in garlic, chili powder, tomatillos, beans, and 8 cups (2 quarts) water; season very generously with salt (about 2 teaspoons). Cover and bring to a boil.

2 / Lower heat to slowly simmer chili, uncovered and stirring occasionally, until beans are just cooked through but firm, about 1 hour. Raise heat to quickly simmer chili, uncovered and stirring occasionally, until beans just begin to break apart and broth has reduced to a thick, flavorful gravy, about 1 hour. Stir in cilantro. Season chili with additional salt to taste.

tomatillo lanterns
summer lighting
the garden path

Split Pea Soup with Roasted Kale

Split Pea Soup with Roasted Kale

If you want to be fancy, reserve a pinch of the crispy kale to scatter on top of each serving.

Makes about 6 bowlfuls (or 2½ quarts)

---

1 medium bunch kale (curly preferred), trimmed of thick stems and ribs, chopped (about 6 packed cups)
2 tablespoons plus ½ cup olive oil, divided
Kosher salt and freshly ground black pepper
6 cloves garlic, peeled, smashed with knife
1 medium onion, chopped
2 celery stalks, chopped
2 medium carrots, peeled and sliced into ½-inch disks
2 tablespoons mustard seeds or 1 tablespoon ground mustard
¼ cup nutritional yeast
2 teaspoons smoked paprika
2 bay leaves, fresh or dried
⅛ teaspoon freshly grated nutmeg
1 pound green or yellow split peas
1 tablespoon cider vinegar

1 / Heat broiler with rack about 5 inches away from heat. On a large rimmed baking sheet, drizzle kale with 2 tablespoons oil; season generously with salt and pepper (about 1 teaspoon salt and ½ teaspoon pepper). Use hands to scrunch and squeeze oil and seasoning into greens (they will wilt and soften as you work). Broil greens, tossing every 2 minutes, until charred at the edges, about 6 minutes. (You should have about 2 cups roasted kale.)

2 / In a large, heavy pot, heat remaining oil over medium heat until hot. Tip pan to pool oil at one side; add garlic to oil. Cook, turning often, until garlic is evenly golden brown, about 2 minutes. Add onion, celery, and carrot; season generously with salt and pepper (about 1 teaspoon salt and ½ teaspoon pepper). Cook, stirring often, until vegetables have softened, about 10 minutes. Stir in mustard seeds, yeast, paprika, bay leaves, and nutmeg. Cook, stirring, until spices are thick and fragrant, about 2 minutes. Stir in reserved roasted kale, split peas, and 8 cups (2 quarts) water; season generously with salt (about 1 teaspoon). Cover and bring to a boil.

3 / Lower heat to slowly simmer soup, uncovered and stirring occasionally, until thickened to desired consistency and flavors have blended, about 1½ hours. Stir in vinegar. Season soup with additional salt and vinegar to taste. Remove bay leaves before serving.

ebb tide
scraping
my bowl

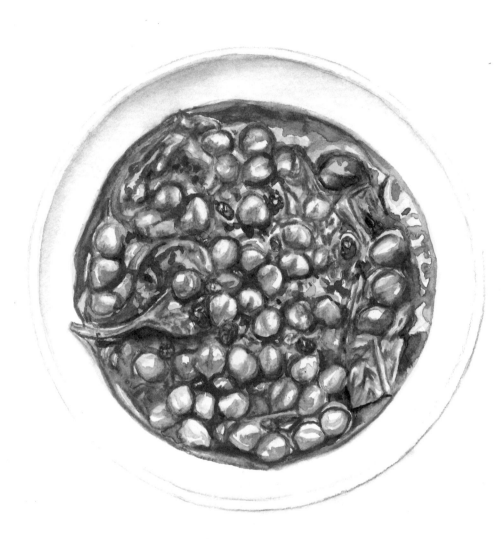

Catalan Chickpea Stew with Spinach

Catalan Chickpea Stew with Spinach

Serve this with a Spanish fried egg—a soft yolk surrounded by a halo of crisp bubbles, drenched in olive oil—if you're into that sort of thing.

Makes about 8 bowlfuls (or 2 quarts)

¾ cup olive oil
6 cloves garlic, peeled
½ cup parsley leaves, well-dried
¼ cup pine nuts
1 (1-ounce) slice gluten-free sandwich bread, coarsely grated (about ½ cup crumbs)
1 large onion, chopped
Kosher salt and freshly ground black pepper
¼ cup tomato paste
1 tablespoon smoked paprika
1 pound dried chickpeas, soaked overnight
½ cup currants
2 teaspoons sherry or cider vinegar, plus more to taste
5 cups baby spinach (5-ounce container)

1 / In a large, heavy pot, heat oil over medium heat until hot. Add garlic, parsley, pine nuts, and bread crumbs. Cook, stirring often, until pine nuts and bread crumbs are a deep golden brown, about 5 minutes. Use a slotted spoon to remove toasted ingredients to a bowl; reserve oil in pot.

2 / Heat reserved pot with oil over medium heat until hot. Add onion; season generously with salt (about 1 teaspoon). Lower heat and cook slowly, stirring occasionally, until onion is shiny, clear, and tender, about 15 minutes. While onion cooks, transfer reserved bread crumb mixture to a food processor; season generously with salt and pepper (about 1 teaspoon salt and ½ teaspoon pepper). Blend bread crumb mixture until smooth to make a picada. Stir tomato paste, paprika, and picada into onion. Add chickpeas and 8 cups (2 quarts) water to pot; season very generously with salt (about 2 teaspoons). Cover and bring to a boil.

3 / Lower heat to slowly simmer stew, uncovered and stirring occasionally, until chickpeas are just cooked through but firm, about 1 hour. Stir in currants. Raise heat to quickly simmer stew, stirring occasionally, until chickpeas are soft and broth has reduced to a thick, flavorful gravy, about 1 hour. Add vinegar. Stir in spinach by the handful. Season stew with additional salt and vinegar to taste.

thunder rolls
the earthy crunch
of chickpeas

Kinda Tortilla Soup

Kinda Tortilla Soup

If you're a fan of corn (or tradition), stir in frozen corn when the soup's done and pile your bowl high with crushed tortilla chips.

Makes about 8 bowlfuls (or 2 quarts)

¼ cup hulled millet or coarse cornmeal (sometimes called "polenta")
1 large onion, quartered
6 cloves garlic, peeled
4 Anaheim or poblano peppers (about 1 pound)
Kosher salt
¼ cup avocado oil
1 large green bell pepper, chopped
2 tablespoons tomato paste
¼ cup Toasted Chili Powder (page 163) or 2 tablespoons
     store-bought
1 cup dried black beans, soaked overnight
2 tablespoons firmly packed chopped cilantro leaves
1 tablespoon freshly squeezed lime juice, plus more to taste
Sliced ripe avocado for serving

1 / Heat a small, heavy skillet (such as cast-iron) over medium-high heat until hot (without oil); add millet. Roast, tossing, until millet is dark golden brown and fragrant, about 10 minutes. Transfer to a spice grinder and blend until finely ground. (You should have ⅓ cup ground millet.)

2 / Heat broiler with rack about 5 inches from heat. On a large rimmed baking sheet, arrange onion, garlic, and whole Anaheim peppers in a single layer. Broil vegetables, turning once, until onions are charred and peppers are blistered in spots, about 10 minutes. Set aside until peppers are cool enough to handle, about 10 minutes; remove skins, stems, and seeds from peppers. Transfer vegetables to a blender jar with 1 cup water; blend, cracking lid and covering with a towel to release steam, until smooth. Season salsa mixture very generously with salt (about 2 teaspoons). Place blender jar next to stove.

3 / Heat oil in a large, heavy pot over medium heat until hot. Add bell pepper; season generously with salt (about 1 teaspoon). Cook, stirring often, until pepper has softened, about 8 minutes. Stir in tomato paste, chili powder, and ground millet until combined. Add beans, reserved salsa mixture, and 8 cups (2 quarts) water; season generously with salt (about 1 teaspoon). Cover and bring to a boil.

4 / Lower heat to slowly simmer soup, uncovered and stirring occasionally, until beans are tender but not falling apart and broth has reduced to a thick gravy, about 1½ hours. Stir in cilantro and lime juice. Season soup with additional salt and lime juice to taste. Serve soup with sliced avocado.

summer heat
licking the Guajillo
from his lips

Thanksgiving Soup

Thanksgiving Soup

The carnivores at your table can add shredded leftover turkey to this soup; it can be our little secret that it tastes like the holidays without it.

Makes about 10 bowlfuls (or 3 quarts)

1 large parsnip, peeled and cut into 1-inch disks
1 large carrot, peeled and cut into 1-inch disks
1 small celery root, peeled and cut into 1-inch pieces
1 small acorn squash, seeds removed and cut into 2-inch pieces (do not peel)
¼ teaspoon ground nutmeg
2 tablespoons olive oil, divided
Kosher salt and freshly ground black pepper
10 sage leaves, finely chopped
1 leek, white part only, halved lengthwise and sliced into ½-inch pieces
2 celery stalks, chopped
¼ cup nutritional yeast
1 cup wild rice, rinsed if desired
1 tablespoon cider vinegar, plus more to taste
Roasted hazelnuts, chopped, for serving, optional

1 / Heat broiler with rack about 5 inches from heat. On a large rimmed baking sheet, toss parsnip, carrot, celery root, and squash with nutmeg and 1 tablespoon oil; season with salt and pepper (about ½ teaspoon salt and ¼ teaspoon pepper). Broil vegetables until browned in spots yet firm when pierced, about 8 minutes. While vegetables broil, combine sage leaves and 1 tablespoon salt in a mortar; use a pestle to smash and grind salt and sage together until it forms greenish grit. (Alternatively, add salt to pile of chopped sage leaves on a cutting board; chop and use side of knife to smash salt and sage together.)

2 / Heat remaining oil in a large, heavy pot over medium heat until hot. Add leek and celery; season generously with salt (about 1 teaspoon). Cook, stirring often, until vegetables have softened, about 10 minutes. Stir in yeast, rice, reserved vegetables and sage salt, and 8 cups (2 quarts) water. Cover and bring to a boil. Lower heat to slowly simmer soup, covered and without stirring, until rice is tender, about 45 minutes. Stir in vinegar. Season soup with additional salt and vinegar to taste. Serve soup topped with hazelnuts, if desired.

night prayer
holding our hands
around a warm bowl

Ethiopian Lentil Soup

Ethiopian Lentil Soup

Stir in some fresh spinach at the end of cooking if you miss your veggies. (They miss you, too.)

Makes about 8 bowlfuls (or 2 quarts)

½ cup Vegan Nit'r Qibe (page 164) or coconut oil
1 medium onion, chopped
2 cloves garlic, finely chopped
Kosher salt
1 (14.5-ounce) can diced tomatoes
2 cups dried red lentils
2 teaspoons Homemade Berbere (page 164) or store-bought
1 tablespoon freshly squeezed lemon juice, plus more to taste
Cilantro leaves for serving, optional

1 / Heat nit'r qibe in a large, heavy pot over medium heat until hot. Add onion and garlic; season generously with salt (about 1 teaspoon). Lower heat and cook slowly until onion is shiny, clear, and tender, about 15 minutes. Stir in tomatoes, lentils, berbere, and 8 cups (2 quarts) water; season generously with salt (about 1 teaspoon). Cover and bring to a boil.

2 / Lower heat to slowly simmer soup, uncovered and stirring occasionally, until thickened and lentils are tender, about 45 minutes. Stir in lemon juice. Season soup with additional salt and lemon juice to taste. Serve soup topped with cilantro leaves, if desired.

forest green
tin mug
drifting mountain mist

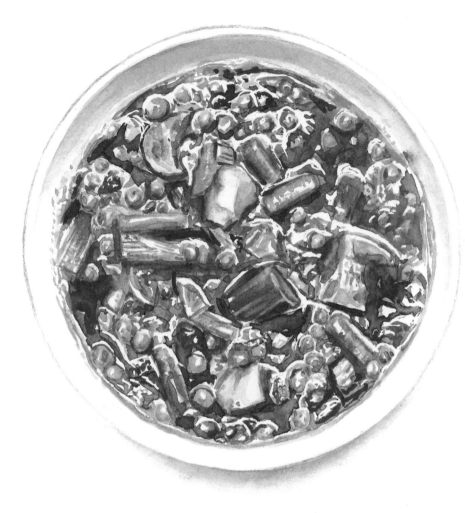

Chunky Garden Vegetable Stew

Chunky Garden Vegetable Stew

This hearty classic American vegetable stew is one part canned nostalgia and one part hippie nutrition. The result is a comforting, nutrient-dense meal in a bowl.

Makes about 8 bowlfuls (or 4 quarts)

¼ cup olive oil
1 medium onion, chopped
2 celery stalks, cut into 1-inch pieces
2 cloves garlic, chopped
Kosher salt and freshly ground black pepper
1 bay leaf, fresh or dried
½ teaspoon dried turmeric
2 tablespoons nutritional yeast
1 (28-ounce) can crushed tomatoes
8 ounces green beans, cut into 1-inch pieces (about 2 cups)
1 medium white sweet potato, peeled and cut into 1-inch pieces (about 2 cups)
3 large carrots, peeled and sliced 1-inch chunks (about 3 cups)
1 cup dried mung beans
1 medium yellow squash, quartered lengthwise and sliced into 1-inch chunks
1 cup frozen peas
1 tablespoon cider vinegar, plus more to taste

1 / Heat oil in a large, heavy pot over medium heat until hot; add onion, celery, and garlic. Season with salt and pepper (about 1 teaspoon salt and ½ teaspoon pepper). Cook, stirring often, until onion has softened, about 10 minutes. Stir in bay leaf, turmeric, yeast, tomatoes, beans, potato, carrots, mung beans, and 6 cups (1½ quarts) water; season generously with salt (about 2 teaspoons). Cover and bring to a boil.

2 / Lower heat and simmer, uncovered and stirring occasionally, until mung beans are just tender, about 25 minutes. Add squash and frozen peas; simmer until squash is tender but still crisp, about 5 minutes. Stir in vinegar. Season soup with additional vinegar and salt to taste. Remove bay leaf before serving.

family soup night
its lingering warmth
decades later

Fennel Farinata

Fennel Farinata

This is a vegan adaptation of a recipe from my first cookbook, *Twenty-Dollar, Twenty-Minute Meals*. It likes cheese, but if you don't, top servings with capers fried in olive oil.

Makes about 8 bowlfuls (or 2 quarts)

½ cup hulled millet or coarse cornmeal (sometimes called "polenta")
¼ cup olive oil
1 medium onion, chopped
2 celery stalks, chopped
1 medium carrot, peeled and chopped
1 small fennel bulb (with fronds preferred), cored and chopped (fronds, optional, reserved)
2 cloves garlic, chopped
Kosher salt and freshly ground black pepper
2 bay leaves, fresh or dried
1 cup dried chickpeas, soaked overnight
1 small bunch kale, ribs and stems removed, thinly sliced
2 tablespoons chopped parsley leaves
1 tablespoon freshly squeezed lemon juice, plus more to taste

1 / Pour millet into a blender jar or spice grinder. Process until millet is about halfway ground. (Test this by rubbing some of the mixture between your fingers; it should feel coarse, but your fingers should be powdery. You should have about ½ cup ground millet.)

2 / Heat oil in a large, heavy pot over medium heat until hot. Add onion, celery, carrot, fennel, and garlic; season very generously with salt and pepper (about 2 teaspoons salt and ½ teaspoon pepper). Cook, stirring often, until vegetables have softened, about 10 minutes. While vegetables cook, if using fennel fronds, finely chop enough to make 2 tablespoons; set aside. Stir in reserved millet, bay leaves, chickpeas, kale, and 8 cups (2 quarts) water; season generously with salt (about 1 teaspoon). Cover and bring to a boil.

3 / Lower heat to slowly simmer soup, uncovered and stirring often, until chickpeas are tender, about 1½ hours. Stir in reserved fennel fronds (if using), parsley, and lemon juice. Season soup with additional salt and lemon juice to taste. Remove bay leaves before serving.

cold weather comfort
the big dipper
ladling the moon

Greek Soup Mashup

Greek Soup Mashup

This soup is a fantasy blend of three of my favorite traditional Greek soups—avgolemono, fasolada, and tahinosoupa—to create a kind of Greek soup unicorn. Add feta if you dare.

Makes about 6 bowlfuls (or 2 quarts)

¼ cup olive oil
1 large onion, chopped
3 celery stalks, chopped
3 medium carrots, peeled and chopped
4 cloves garlic, finely chopped
Kosher salt and freshly ground black pepper
1 teaspoon dried oregano
2 tablespoons nutritional yeast
¾ cup short-grain brown rice
1 cup dried navy beans, soaked overnight
¼ cup well-stirred tahini
¼ cup firmly packed chopped dill fronds
1 lemon

1 / Heat oil in a large, heavy pot over medium heat until hot. Add onion, celery, carrots, and garlic; season generously with salt and pepper (about 1 teaspoon salt and ½ teaspoon pepper). Cook, stirring often, until vegetables have softened, about 10 minutes. Stir in oregano, yeast, rice, beans, and 8 cups (2 quarts) water; season very generously with salt (about 2 teaspoons). Cover and bring to a boil.

2 / Lower heat to slowly simmer soup, covered and without stirring, until beans and rice are tender, about 1 hour. Place tahini in a medium bowl; whisk in enough broth until the mixture is the texture of a milkshake. Stir tahini mixture into soup with dill. Finely grate zest of lemon over soup (about 1 teaspoon); squeeze juice into soup (about 2 tablespoons). Season soup with additional salt and pepper to taste.

stacked bowls
after dinner
spooning

Hoppin' John

Hoppin' John

Southerners will tell you that this stew might bring you some luck in the New Year if it's eaten on New Year's Day. (Over rice. With or without pepper sauce. However you want!)

Makes about 8 bowlfuls (or 2½ quarts)

---

1 (7-ounce) can chipotle chiles in adobo
8 sprigs thyme
1 tablespoon smoked paprika
2 bay leaves, fresh or dried
½ cup olive oil
1 large onion, chopped
1 large green bell pepper, chopped
1 medium carrot, peeled and chopped
Kosher salt
1 small bunch collard greens, ribs and stems removed, cut into 1-inch ribbons (about 5 cups)
1 pound dried black-eyed peas, soaked overnight
1 (14.5-ounce) can fire-roasted diced tomatoes
2 tablespoons cider vinegar, plus more to taste
Cooked rice for serving

1 / Remove 1 chipotle chile from can; remove stems (and seeds, for less heat) and chop. Place chopped chile in a small bowl with 2 tablespoons adobo sauce. (Transfer remaining chiles and sauce to storage container; reserve for another use.) Add thyme, paprika, and bay leaves to small bowl with chile and sauce; set aside.

2 / Heat oil in a large, heavy pot over medium heat until hot. Add onion, bell pepper, and carrot; season generously with salt (about 1 teaspoon). Cook, stirring often, until vegetables have softened, about 10 minutes. Stir in collards, beans, tomatoes, reserved spices, and 8 cups (2 quarts) water; season very generously with salt (about 2 teaspoons). Cover and bring to a boil.

3 / Lower heat to slowly simmer stew, covered and without stirring, until beans and greens are tender but still a bit crisp, about 1 hour. Raise heat to quickly simmer stew, stirring occasionally, until beans just begin to break apart, greens are soft, and broth has reduced to a thick, flavorful gravy, about 30 minutes. Stir in vinegar. Season stew with additional salt and vinegar to taste. Remove thyme sprigs and bay leaves before serving. Serve over rice.

New Year's Day
counting our blessings
bowls full

Minestrone Invernale

Minestrone Invernale

If you eat cheese, add a 4-inch piece of Parmesan rind with the greens and remove with the rosemary sprigs in the final step. It can be our tasty little secret.

Makes about 12 bowlfuls (or 3 quarts)

2 heads garlic
4 sprigs rosemary, divided
¼ cup olive oil, divided
Kosher salt and freshly ground black pepper
1 medium onion, chopped
2 inner celery stalks with their leaves, chopped
2 medium carrots, peeled and chopped
1 small bunch Swiss chard, leaves shredded (4 cups) and stems roughly chopped (about 1 cup)
2 tablespoons Dijon mustard
1 cup dried cranberry or pinto beans, soaked overnight
1 (14.5-ounce) can diced tomatoes
1 small head radicchio, halved, cored, and shredded (about 4 cups)
1 small bunch Lacinato kale, ribs and stems removed, roughly torn (about 2 cups)
1 cup rotini pasta (gluten-free or traditional), chopped or broken into small pieces

1 / Preheat oven to 350°F. Slice into heads of garlic crosswise, removing the topmost ¾ inch to just expose the raw cloves. Place garlic on a double thickness of aluminum foil (lined with parchment, if desired) with 1 sprig rosemary. Drizzle garlic with 1 tablespoon olive oil and season with salt and pepper (about ½ teaspoon salt and ¼ teaspoon pepper). Gather edges of foil to enclose garlic and rosemary; place packet on a rimmed baking sheet. Bake until packet is fragrant and sizzling and the cloves are golden and risen from their papers, about 1½ hours. Set aside until cool enough to handle, about 20 minutes. Squeeze garlic from their papers into a small bowl. (You should have about ⅓ cup garlic paste.)

2 / Heat remaining oil in a large, heavy pot over medium heat until hot. Add onion, celery, carrots, and chard stems; season generously with salt and pepper (about 1 teaspoon salt and ½ teaspoon pepper). Cook, stirring often, until vegetables have softened, about 10 minutes. Stir in reserved garlic, mustard, beans, tomatoes, 8 cups (2 quarts) water, remaining rosemary sprigs, and half each chard leaves (2 cups), radicchio (2 cups), and kale (1 cup). Season very generously with salt (about 2 teaspoons). Cover and bring to a boil.

3 / Lower heat to slowly simmer soup, covered and without stirring, until beans are tender, about 1½ hours. Remove from heat; stir in remaining greens and pasta. Let stand, covered, until pasta and greens are softened, about 20 minutes. Remove rosemary sprigs before serving. Season soup with additional salt to taste.

Minestrone Invernale
breaking bread
not resolutions

Jamaican Pumpkin + Red Pea Soup

Jamaican Pumpkin + Red Pea Soup

For added flair when serving, reserve some of the coconut cream listed in the recipe and pour it over the servings before bringing the bowls to the table.

Makes about 8 bowlfuls (or 3 quarts)

4 cloves garlic, peeled
1 jalapeño, seeds and membrane removed for less heat, roughly chopped
1 (1-inch) piece fresh ginger, peeled if desired
1 bunch scallions (both whites and greens), chopped
1 medium onion, quartered
1 teaspoon ground allspice
1 teaspoon ground cinnamon
1 small bunch thyme, stripped (about 2 teaspoons leaves)
Kosher salt and freshly ground black pepper
¼ cup coconut oil
1 cup dried small red beans, soaked overnight
2 medium carrots, peeled and cut into 1-inch pieces
1 small bunch collard greens, ribs and stems removed, sliced into 1-inch strips (about 5 cups)
½ medium calabaza, hubbard, or kabocha squash (about 3½ pounds), peeled, seeds removed, and cut into very large (3-inch) chunks
1 cup full-fat coconut cream (from a well-shaken carton, such as Aroy-D brand; sold at Asian markets)
1 tablespoon coconut sugar
2 tablespoons freshly squeezed lime juice, plus more to taste
Lime wedges for serving

1 / In a blender jar, combine garlic, jalapeño, ginger, scallions, onion, allspice, cinnamon, thyme, ½ teaspoon black pepper, and ¼ cup water; blend until smooth. Place blender jar next to stove.

2 / Heat oil in a large, heavy pot over medium heat until melted and hot. Add aromatic purée (it will spatter); season very generously with salt (about 2 teaspoons). Cook, stirring, until purée thickens and is fragrant, about 5 minutes. Stir in beans, carrots, collards, squash, and 8 cups (2 quarts) water; season very generously with salt (about 2 teaspoons). Cover and bring to a boil.

3 / Lower heat to slowly simmer soup, uncovered without stirring, until beans and pumpkin are tender, about 45 minutes. Gently stir in coconut cream, coconut sugar, and lime juice, taking care not to break apart squash. Season soup with additional salt and lime juice to taste. Serve soup with lime wedges.

first snow
the shape of a gourd
on my front steps

Golden Borscht

Golden Borscht

If you are lucky enough to find beets with greens, don't throw them away! Wash them, remove their ribs and stems, and slice them into 1-inch ribbons; add them to the stew along with the cabbage.

Makes about 8 bowlfuls (or 2 quarts)

¼ cup olive oil
1 small onion, chopped
2 celery stalks, chopped
1 clove garlic, chopped
Kosher salt and freshly ground black pepper
1 teaspoon caraway seeds
¼ teaspoon ground turmeric, optional
1 pound carrots (about 6 medium), peeled and cut into 1-inch pieces
1 pound yellow beets (about 2 medium), peeled and cut into 1-inch chunks
1 pound white sweet potato (about 1 large), cut into 2-inch chunks
½ small Savoy or green cabbage, cored and cut into 1-inch pieces (about 4 cups)
1 bay leaf, fresh or dried
¼ cup cider vinegar, plus more to taste
¼ cup firmly packed chopped dill fronds
¼ cup firmly packed chopped parsley leaves
Sour cream or Greek yogurt for serving, optional

1 / Heat oil in a large, heavy pot over medium heat until hot. Add onion, celery, and garlic; season generously with salt and pepper (about 1 teaspoon salt and ½ teaspoon pepper). Cook, stirring often, until vegetables are softened but not browned, about 10 minutes. Stir in caraway and turmeric (if using). Stir in carrots, beets, potato, cabbage, bay leaf, vinegar, and 6 cups (1½ quarts) water; season very generously with salt (about 2 teaspoons). Cover and bring to a boil.

2 / Lower heat to slowly simmer stew, uncovered and without stirring, until beets and cabbage are just tender, about 30 minutes. Stir in dill and parsley. Season stew with additional salt and vinegar to taste. Remove bay leaf before serving. Serve stew topped with a generous dollop of sour cream or Greek yogurt, if desired.

golden borscht
the long stretch
of grandma's smile

Cowboy Chili

Cowboy Chili

If we can imagine together a vegan hipster cowboy, this soup would be his campfire meal.

Makes about 8 bowlfuls (or 2½ quarts)

¼ cup ground chicory or decaf coffee
2 tablespoons molasses
1 large onion, chopped
1 large green bell pepper, chopped
¼ cup avocado oil
4 cloves garlic, chopped
3 tablespoons Toasted Chili Powder (page 163) or
    2 tablespoons store-bought
¼ cup nutritional yeast
2 tablespoons unsweetened carob or cocoa powder
1 tablespoon smoked paprika
1 (28-ounce) can crushed tomatoes
1 cup dried black beans, soaked overnight
1 cup dried small red beans, soaked overnight
Kosher salt
1 tablespoon cider vinegar, plus more to taste
Cornbread for serving

1 / In a liquid measuring cup, combine chicory and 2 cups boiling water; stir in molasses. Set aside.

2 / Heat a large, heavy pot over high heat until very hot (do not add oil); add onion and bell pepper in a single layer. Cook, without stirring, until vegetables are charred around edges, about 8 minutes. Stir in oil, garlic, chili powder, yeast, carob, and paprika until combined. Add tomatoes, black and red beans, and 6 cups (1½ quarts) water. Strain brewed chicory mixture into pot through a fine-mesh sieve lined with cheesecloth or single sheet of damp paper towel; season very generously with salt (about 2 teaspoons). Stir to combine. Cover and bring to a boil.

3 / Lower heat to slowly simmer simmer chili, uncovered and stirring occasionally, until beans are just cooked through but still firm, about 45 minutes. Raise heat to quickly simmer chili, stirring occasionally to break apart the beans, until beans are soft and broth has reduced to a thick, flavorful gravy, about 30 minutes. Stir in vinegar. Season chili with additional salt and vinegar to taste. Serve chili with cornbread.

mouths full ... the fire crackles

Harira

Harira

Put on *Casablanca* and a cozy sweater, and slurp this soup from the couch for some seriously comforting Moroccan vibes.

Makes about 8 bowlfuls (or 3 quarts)

½ cup olive oil
1 medium onion, chopped
1 (1-inch) piece fresh ginger, peeled and chopped
Kosher salt
1 teaspoon dried turmeric
1 (3-inch) piece cinnamon stick
1 (14.5-ounce) can diced tomatoes
1 cup dried chickpeas, soaked overnight
1 cup dried green (French) lentils
½ cup long-grain brown rice
2 tablespoons tomato paste
2 tablespoons chickpea flour (sometimes called "besan")
    or all-purpose flour
¼ cup chopped cilantro leaves
2 tablespoons freshly squeezed lemon juice, plus more
    to taste

1 / In a large, heavy pot, heat oil over medium heat until hot. Add onion and ginger; season generously with salt (about 1 teaspoon). Lower heat and cook slowly, stirring often, until vegetables are a light golden brown, about 15 minutes. Stir in turmeric, cinnamon, tomatoes, chickpeas, lentils, rice, and 6 cups (1½ quarts) water; season very generously with salt (about 2 teaspoons). Cover and bring to a boil.

2 / Lower heat to slowly simmer soup, covered and without stirring, until chickpeas and lentils are just tender, about 1 hour. While soup simmers, whisk together tomato paste, flour, cilantro, lemon juice, and ¼ cup water in a small bowl; season generously with salt (about 1 teaspoon). Raise heat to quickly simmer soup; whisk in flour mixture. Simmer soup until broth becomes cloudy and thickens, about 5 minutes. Season soup with additional salt and lemon juice to taste. Remove cinnamon stick before serving.

soup bowl
filled with promise
new moon

Gumbo Z'Herbes

Gumbo Z'Herbes

If zydeco music could drown in mustard greens and okra, this is what it would taste like. Alternate title: Carnival in a Bowl.

Makes about 8 bowlfuls (or 2 quarts)

¼ cup olive oil
¼ cup chickpea flour (sometimes called "besan")
1 large onion, chopped
1 large green bell pepper, chopped
2 celery stalks, chopped
6 cloves garlic, finely chopped
Kosher salt
2 tablespoons Homemade Cajun Seasoning (page 165) or store-bought
2 bay leaves, fresh or dried
1 pound fresh or frozen okra, cut into 1-inch pieces
1 small bunch mustard greens, ribs and stems removed, roughly torn (about 4 cups)
1 bunch parsley (including stems), chopped
1 tablespoon cider vinegar, plus more to taste
5 cups baby spinach (5-ounce container)
Cooked rice for serving, optional

1 / In a large, heavy pot, heat oil over medium heat until hot. Add flour and cook, stirring constantly, until it turns a deep coppery brown, about 12 minutes. Stir in onion, bell pepper, celery, and garlic; season generously with salt (about 1 teaspoon). (The floured vegetables will stick a little but should not scorch; if scorching, turn down the heat.) Cook, stirring often, until vegetables have softened, about 10 minutes.

2 / Add Cajun seasoning, bay leaves, okra, mustard greens, parsley, and 8 cups (2 quarts) water; season very generously with salt (about 2 teaspoons). Cover and bring to a boil.

3 / Lower heat to slowly simmer stew, uncovered and stirring occasionally, until greens and okra are very soft, okra has broken apart, and broth has reduced to a thick gravy, about 40 minutes. Add vinegar; stir in spinach by the handful. Season stew with additional salt and vinegar to taste. Remove bay leaves before serving. Serve stew over rice, if desired.

slurping gumbo
French Quarter
moon

Louisiana Red Bean Soup

—————•—————

Louisiana Red Bean Soup

Help these beans find their other half—rice—and top with all the tasty roasted vegetables you can find.

Makes about 6 bowlfuls (or 2 quarts)

---

1 (7-ounce) can chipotle chiles in adobo
½ cup avocado oil
1 large onion, chopped
2 celery stalks, chopped
1 large green bell pepper, chopped
4 cloves garlic, finely chopped
Kosher salt
2 tablespoons Homemade Cajun Seasoning (page 165)
    or store-bought
1 tablespoon smoked paprika
2 bay leaves, fresh or dried
1 pound dried small red beans, soaked overnight
1 tablespoon cider vinegar, plus more to taste
Cooked rice for serving

1 / Remove 1 chipotle chile from can; remove stems (and seeds, for less heat) and chop. Place chile in small bowl with 2 tablespoons adobo sauce. (Transfer remaining chiles and sauce to storage container; reserve for another use.)

2 / Heat oil in a large, heavy pot over medium heat until hot. Add onion, celery, bell pepper, and garlic; season generously with salt (about 1 teaspoon). Cook, stirring often, until vegetables have softened, about 10 minutes. Stir in reserved chile, Cajun seasoning, paprika, bay leaves, beans, and 8 cups (2 quarts) water; season generously with salt (about 1 teaspoon). Cover and bring to a boil.

3 / Lower heat to slowly simmer soup, uncovered and stirring occasionally, until beans are just cooked through but firm, about 1 hour. Raise heat to quickly simmer soup, uncovered and stirring occasionally, until beans just begin to break apart and broth has reduced to a thick, flavorful gravy, about 30 minutes. Stir in vinegar. Season soup with additional salt and vinegar to taste. Remove bay leaves before serving. Serve soup over rice.

Ash Wednesday
still draped in beads
grinning Buddha

Nearly Retro Cabbage Soup

Nearly Retro Cabbage Soup

This girl is a rebel: both chunky and funky when compared to the classic. No fad diet or body shame here.

Makes about 8 bowlfuls (or 2½ quarts)

½ cup coconut oil
1 medium head green cabbage, quartered (core intact)
Kosher salt and freshly ground black pepper
1 medium onion, chopped
2 celery stalks, sliced ½ inch thick
4 cloves garlic, finely chopped
1 (1-inch) piece fresh ginger, peeled and chopped
2 tablespoons tomato paste
2 medium carrots, peeled and cut into 1-inch pieces
8 ounces Brussels sprouts, halved (or quartered if large)
1 cup dried butter beans, soaked overnight
1 (14.5-ounce) can fire-roasted diced tomatoes
1 tablespoon coconut aminos, plus more to taste
1 tablespoon freshly squeezed lemon juice, plus more to taste

1 / Heat oil in a large, heavy pot over high heat until very hot (it will smoke). Sear cabbage in batches until it's a deep caramel color on both sides, about 10 minutes. Transfer cabbage to a cutting board to cool 5 minutes; season with salt and pepper (about ½ teaspoon each salt and pepper). Reserve oil and pan.

2 / While cabbage cools, lower heat under pot to medium. Add onion, celery, garlic, and ginger; season generously with salt (about 1 teaspoon). Cook, stirring often, until vegetables have softened, about 10 minutes. While vegetables cook, slice away core of cabbage and cut into 2-inch pieces. Stir tomato paste into pot with vegetables. Add carrots, Brussels sprouts, beans, tomatoes, reserved cabbage, and 6 cups (1½ quarts) water; season very generously with salt (about 2 teaspoons). Cover and bring to a boil.

3 / Lower heat to slowly simmer soup, covered and without stirring, until cabbage and beans are tender, about 1 hour. Stir in coconut aminos and lemon juice. Season soup with additional salt and lemon juice to taste.

soup diet
happily becoming
what we eat

West African Vegetable Stew

West African Vegetable Stew

This is a choose-your-own-adventure style of a traditional Senegalese peanut stew. Because friends don't let friends' throats close up.

Makes about 8 bowlfuls (or 2½ quarts)

¼ cup avocado oil
1 medium onion, chopped
4 cloves garlic, chopped
1 (1-inch) piece fresh ginger, peeled and chopped
Kosher salt
2 tablespoons Homemade Curry Powder (page 162) or store-bought
⅛ teaspoon cayenne pepper
1 (28-ounce) can diced tomatoes
1 small bunch collard greens, ribs and stems removed, sliced into 1-inch strips (about 5 cups)
4 small (4 to 6-ounce) sweet potatoes or yams, peeled
8 ounces green beans, cut into 1-inch pieces (about 2 cups)
½ cup unsweetened sunflower seed, cashew, or peanut butter
1 cup roasted sunflower seeds, cashews, or peanuts, divided
1 tablespoon freshly squeezed lemon juice, plus more to taste

1 / Heat oil in a large, heavy pot over medium heat until hot. Add onion, garlic, and ginger; season generously with salt (about 1 teaspoon). Cook, stirring often, until vegetables have softened, about 10 minutes. Stir in curry powder, cayenne, tomatoes, collards, and 6 cups (1½ quarts) water; season very generously with salt (about 2 teaspoons). Cover and bring to a boil. Add whole potatoes and beans to pot.

2 / Lower heat to slowly simmer stew, covered and without stirring, until potatoes are just tender when pierced with a knife, about 30 minutes. In a blender jar, combine 1 cooked potato, 1 cup broth, and sunflower seed butter; blend until smooth. Stir seed butter mixture into stew with ½ cup sunflower seeds and lemon juice. (Stew will thicken slightly and become creamy.) Season stew with additional lemon juice and salt to taste. Break potatoes into large chunks before serving. Serve stew topped with a handful of sunflower seeds (or stir full amount into pot before serving).

new city
new soup
old crows

Persian Herb and Noodle Soup

Persian Herb and Noodle Soup

This is my take on Ash Reshteh, a traditional soup made for Persian New Year that celebrates the arrival of spring. Serve with or without the dollop of dairy.

Makes about 8 bowlfuls (or 3 quarts)

½ cup olive oil
1 medium onion, chopped
4 cloves garlic, finely chopped
Kosher salt and freshly ground black pepper
¼ cup nutritional yeast
1 teaspoon dried turmeric
1 cup dried navy beans, soaked overnight
½ cup dried brown lentils
5 cups baby spinach (5-ounce container), roughly chopped
2 bunches parsley (stems included), roughly chopped
2 bunches cilantro (stems included), roughly chopped
1 large bunch dill (fronds only), roughly chopped
2 large (1-inch-thick) bunches chives, roughly chopped
1 cup mint leaves (stripped from about 15 sprigs), chopped
8 ounces spaghetti (gluten-free or traditional), broken in half
2 tablespoons freshly squeezed lemon juice, plus more to taste
Greek yogurt for serving, optional

1 / Heat oil in a large, heavy pot over medium heat until hot. Add onion and garlic; season generously with salt and pepper (about 1 teaspoon salt and ½ teaspoon pepper). Cook, stirring often, until onion has softened but not browned, about 10 minutes. Stir in yeast and turmeric. Add beans, lentils, spinach, parsley, cilantro, dill, chives, mint, and 8 cups (2 quarts) water; season very generously with salt (about 2 teaspoons). (Pot will be very full.) Cover and bring to a boil.

2 / Lower heat to slowly simmer soup, uncovered and stirring occasionally, until beans are just cooked through but firm, about 1 hour. Scatter pasta over surface and pour 1 cup water over top. Cover pot and raise heat to quickly simmer soup until beans are soft and pasta is cooked through, about 15 minutes. Stir in lemon juice, using spoon to separate cooked noodles. Season soup with additional salt and lemon juice to taste. Serve soup topped with Greek yogurt, if desired.

a long noodle
dwindling at your lips
the distance between us

Mexican Butter Bean Soup

Mexican Butter Bean Soup

Serve with sautéed summer squash and a scattering of cilantro for a new look at Mexican comfort food.

Makes about 8 bowlfuls (or 2 quarts)

1 large onion, quartered
1 (14.5-ounce) can diced tomatoes
4 cloves garlic, peeled
¼ teaspoon saffron threads
½ cup avocado oil
1 teaspoon ground cumin
1 teaspoon ground coriander
Kosher salt and freshly ground black pepper
1 pound dried butter beans, soaked overnight
1 lime

1 / In a blender jar, combine onion and tomatoes; blend until smooth. Place blender jar near stove. Chop garlic and saffron together until garlic and threads are golden and finely chopped.

2 / Heat oil in a large, heavy pot over medium heat until hot. Add garlic mixture, cumin, and coriander. Cook, stirring, until spices are fragrant, about 30 seconds. Stir in onion purée; season generously with salt and pepper (about 1 teaspoon salt and ½ teaspoon pepper). Lower heat to gently simmer, stirring often, until sauce has thickened and turned bright orange, about 10 minutes. Stir in beans and 4 cups (1 quart) water; season very generously with salt (about 2 teaspoons). Cover and bring to a boil.

3 / Lower heat to slowly simmer soup, uncovered and stirring occasionally, until beans are just tender and broth has reduced to a thick, flavorful gravy, about 1 hour. Finely grate 1 teaspoon zest from lime and squeeze from it 1 tablespoon juice; stir both into soup. Season soup with additional salt and lime juice to taste.

the taste of flowers
seasoning
bean stew

Cream of Mushroom Soup

Cream of Mushroom Soup

Be a rebel and combine your soup and salad: toss a small handful of baby arugula and walnuts with olive oil and sherry vinegar and pile it on top of this soup.

Makes about 8 bowlfuls (or 2½ quarts)

---

1 ounce dried porcini mushrooms, chopped or broken into small pieces (about ¾ cup)

⅓ cup nutritional yeast

Kosher salt and freshly ground black pepper

½ cup gluten-free rolled oats

¼ cup olive oil

1 medium onion, chopped

2 cloves garlic, finely chopped

1 pound cremini mushrooms, trimmed of dry stems, quartered (about 4 cups)

8 ounces oyster mushrooms, trimmed of dry stems, roughly chopped (about 3 cups)

8 ounces shiitake mushrooms, trimmed of dry stems, roughly chopped (about 3 cups)

2 sprigs rosemary

2 bay leaves, fresh or dried

½ cup well-stirred tahini

2 teaspoons vegan Worcestershire sauce

1 tablespoon sherry or cider vinegar, plus more to taste

1 / In a blender jar, combine dried mushrooms, yeast, and 1 tablespoon salt; process until finely ground, about 1 minute. Transfer to a bowl and set aside; reserve blender jar. Heat a large, heavy pot over medium heat until hot (without oil); add oats. Roast oats until golden brown and fragrant, about 3 minutes; transfer oats to a bowl and set aside (reserve pot).

2 / Add oil to reserved pot and return to medium heat until hot. Add onion and garlic; season generously with salt and pepper (about 1 teaspoon salt and ½ teaspoon pepper). Cook, stirring often, until onion has softened but not browned, about 10 minutes. Stir in fresh mushrooms; cook until they begin to release their liquid, about 5 minutes. Stir in reserved mushroom salt, rosemary, bay leaves, and 6 cups (1½ quarts) water. Cover and bring to a boil.

3 / Lower heat to slowly simmer soup, uncovered and stirring occasionally, until mushrooms are just tender, about 10 minutes. Remove 2 cups mushroom broth from soup. Transfer broth to reserved blender jar with reserved toasted oats, tahini, and Worcestershire; blend until smooth, about 1 minute. Scrape mixture back into soup. Raise heat to quickly simmer soup, stirring often, until broth is smooth and thick and mushrooms are fully cooked, 5 minutes. Stir in vinegar. Season soup with additional salt and vinegar to taste. Remove rosemary sprigs and bay leaves before serving.

soup can   *taste of comfort*
soup can   *taste of comfort*
soup can   *taste of comfort*

Broccoli and Rice Soup

Broccoli and Rice Soup

Forget the cheesy casserole; eat this soup instead. Top with crushed Ritz crackers for a real win (they're vegan!), or a drizzle of olive oil.

Makes about 8 bowlfuls (or 3 quarts)

1 large bunch broccoli with long stalks (about 1 pound)
½ cup dried mung beans
¼ cup olive oil
1 medium onion, chopped
2 teaspoons ground coriander
Kosher salt and freshly ground black pepper
1 bunch scallions (both whites and greens), chopped
¼ cup nutritional yeast
1 large bunch baby broccoli, sliced into 1-inch pieces (about 5 cups)
½ cup short-grain brown rice
¼ cup cilantro leaves, chopped
1 tablespoon lemon juice, plus more to taste

1 / Cut broccoli to separate stalks from crowns; peel outer, rough layer from stalks with a vegetable peeler and roughly chop. Break and cut broccoli crowns into large florets, about 2 to 3 inches at the widest part. (You should have about 4 cups broccoli florets and 1 to 2 cups chopped broccoli stalks.)

2 / Heat a large, heavy pot over medium heat until hot (without oil); add beans. Roast beans, stirring until evenly golden brown, about 5 minutes. Transfer beans to a parchment-lined baking sheet in a single layer; allow to rest until cool to the touch, about 3 minutes. Use parchment to funnel beans into a spice grinder or blender; process until finely ground. (You should have about ½ cup ground beans.)

3 / Heat oil in reserved pot over medium heat until hot. Add onion and coriander; season generously with salt and pepper (about 1 teaspoon salt and ½ teaspoon pepper). Cook, stirring often, until onion is beginning to soften but not browned, about 5 minutes. Stir in ground beans, reserved broccoli florets and chopped broccoli stalks, scallions, yeast, baby broccoli, rice, and 8 cups (2 quarts) water. Season generously with salt (about 1 teaspoon). Cover and bring to a boil.

4 / Lower heat to slowly simmer soup, uncovered and stirring occasionally, until rice is tender, about 30 minutes. Stir in cilantro and lemon juice. Season soup with additional salt and lemon juice to taste.

mother's casserole
what I didn't like then
I long for now

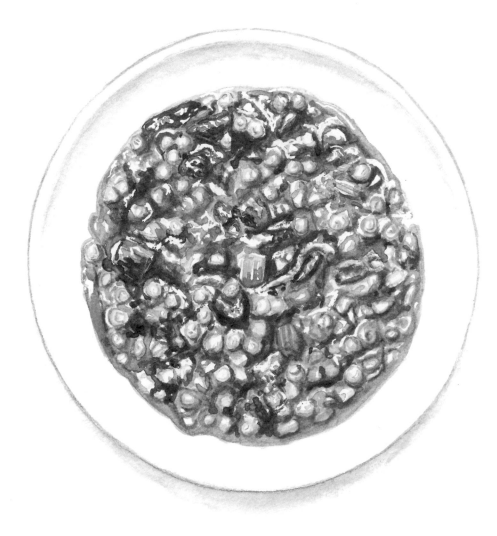

Portuguese Pea Stew

Portuguese Pea Stew

There exists a traditional version of this stew, but this is not it (because: pork). But maybe you can make up for it by serving it topped with an egg like they do in Portugal.

Makes about 8 bowlfuls (or 3 quarts)

1 large red bell pepper
¼ cup olive oil
1 medium onion, chopped
4 cloves garlic, chopped
Kosher salt and freshly ground black pepper
1 tablespoon smoked paprika
1 (4-inch) piece cinnamon stick
1 bay leaf, fresh or dried
1 small bunch cilantro (stems included), chopped
1 cup dried split peas
1 (14.5-ounce) can diced tomatoes
1 (12-ounce) bag frozen peas
1 tablespoon freshly squeezed lemon juice, plus more to taste

1 / Heat broiler with rack about 5 inches away from heat. Place bell pepper directly on rack; broil pepper, turning often, until it is blistered and entirely charred, about 10 minutes. Transfer pepper to a bowl; cover with a plate or pot lid. Set aside until cool enough to handle, about 8 minutes. Remove skin, stem, and seeds from pepper; roughly chop. (You should have about 1 cup chopped roasted pepper.)

2 / Heat oil in a large, heavy pot over medium heat until hot. Add onion and garlic; season generously with salt and pepper (about 1 teaspoon salt and ½ teaspoon pepper). Lower heat and cook, stirring often, until onion is beginning to soften but not browned, about 5 minutes. Stir in reserved roasted pepper, paprika, cinnamon, bay leaf, cilantro, split peas, tomatoes, and 8 cups (2 quarts) water; season very generously with salt (about 2 teaspoons). Cover and bring to a boil.

3 / Lower heat to slowly simmer stew, uncovered and stirring occasionally, until peas are tender and have broken apart and the soup is thick, about 1½ hours. Stir in frozen peas and lemon juice. Season stew with additional salt and lemon juice to taste. Remove bay leaf and cinnamon stick before serving.

pea vines—
clinging
to memories

Peas 'n' Carrots Soup

Peas 'n' Carrots Soup

This is the perennial family-friendly vegetable pair's equivalent of date-night attire—they deserve it after decades in the freezer section.

Makes about 8 bowlfuls (or 3 quarts)

---

8 ounces sugar snap peas, strings discarded, halved
4 large carrots, peeled and cut into 1-inch pieces
4 cloves garlic, sliced
¼ cup olive oil, divided
2 teaspoons ground sumac
Kosher salt and freshly ground black pepper
1 medium onion, chopped
2 celery stalks, chopped
1 (1-inch) piece fresh ginger, peeled and chopped
1 cup dried chickpeas, soaked overnight
1 (14.5-ounce) can fire-roasted diced tomatoes
2 cups frozen green peas
1 tablespoon cider vinegar, plus more to taste
5 cups baby spinach (5-ounce container)

1 / Heat broiler with rack about 5 inches away from heat. On a large rimmed baking sheet, toss snap peas, carrots, and garlic with 1 tablespoon oil and sumac. Season vegetables generously with salt and pepper (about 1 teaspoon salt and ½ teaspoon pepper). Broil vegetables until browned in spots yet firm when pierced, about 4 minutes.

2 / Heat remaining oil in a large, heavy pot over medium heat until hot. Add onion and celery; season generously with salt and pepper (about 1 teaspoon salt and ½ teaspoon pepper). Lower heat and cook slowly, stirring often, until onion is shiny, clear, and tender, about 15 minutes. Stir in ginger, chickpeas, tomatoes, reserved broiled vegetables, and 6 cups (1½ quarts) water; season generously with salt (about 1 teaspoon). Cover and bring to a boil.

3 / Lower heat to slowly simmer soup, uncovered and stirring occasionally, until chickpeas are just cooked through but firm, about 1 hour. Add frozen peas and vinegar. Stir in spinach by the handful. Season soup with additional salt and vinegar to taste.

spring rain
the snap of
peas and carrots

Seattle Springtime Lentil Soup

Seattle Springtime Lentil Soup

This soup is a study in yin and yang: part hearty lentil, part tender spring vegetable, part warm and roasty, part crisp and fresh. Essentially, it's an early spring morning in a bowl.

Makes about 8 bowlfuls (or 2½ quarts)

2 pints cherry tomatoes
4 medium carrots, peeled and sliced into ½-inch disks
1 bunch scallions (both whites and greens), sliced ½ inch thick
¼ cup coconut oil, melted until liquid, divided
Kosher salt
1 (1-inch) piece fresh ginger, peeled and roughly chopped
2 cloves garlic, peeled
1 tablespoon Homemade Curry Powder (page 162) or store-bought
2 tablespoons nigella seeds (sometimes called "kalongi," "black cumin," or "black caraway")
1 (28-ounce) can crushed tomatoes
1 cup dried black lentils
5 cups baby or "wild" arugula (5-ounce container)
1 tablespoon freshly squeezed lime juice, plus more to taste
1 cup full-fat coconut cream (from a well-shaken carton, such as Aroy-D brand; sold at Asian markets)

1 / Preheat oven to 425°F with racks dividing oven into upper and lower thirds. Line 2 large rimmed baking sheets with parchment. Place tomatoes on one prepared baking sheet, and mix carrots and scallions on the other. Drizzle contents of each baking sheet with 1 tablespoon oil and season with salt (about ½ teaspoon per sheet); toss to coat vegetables in oil. Roast vegetables without tossing, swapping the position of pans in oven halfway through, until tomatoes have released their juices and are browned in spots and the carrots are tender when pierced with a knife, about 20 minutes. Transfer ½ cup roasted tomatoes to a bowl; set aside. Use parchment to slide remaining vegetables into a blender with ginger, garlic, and 2 cups water; blend until smooth. Place blender jar next to stove.

2 / Heat remaining oil in a large, heavy pot over medium heat until hot. Add curry powder and nigella seeds and stir until foamy, about 1 minute. Stir in reserved vegetable purée, canned tomatoes, lentils, and 6 cups (1½ quarts) water; season generously with salt (about 1 teaspoon). Cover and bring to a boil.

3 / Lower heat to slowly simmer soup, uncovered and stirring occasionally, until broth is thickened and lentils are tender, about 45 minutes. Stir in arugula, lime juice, and half coconut cream. Season soup with additional salt and lime juice to taste. Serve soup drizzled with remaining coconut cream and topped with a few roasted tomatoes (or stir full amount of cream and tomatoes into pot before serving).

evening birdsong
falling through the chestnut tree
spring rain

Asparagus, Dill + Lemon Soup

Asparagus, Dill + Lemon Soup

This one goes out to the asparagus fans, in a soup that does not resemble baby food.

Makes about 8 bowlfuls (or 2 quarts)

¼ cup olive oil
1 medium leek (white and light green part only), halved lengthwise and sliced
2 celery stalks, chopped
1 medium carrot, peeled and chopped
1 bunch scallions, white and greens chopped separately
Kosher salt
1 medium turnip, peeled and cut into 1-inch pieces
½ small Savoy or green cabbage, cored, quartered, and sliced into ½-inch ribbons
½ cup sorghum, rinsed if desired
1 bunch asparagus (about 1 pound), trimmed of woody ends and cut into 1-inch pieces
1 lemon
¼ cup firmly packed chopped dill fronds
¼ cup firmly packed chopped chervil, optional

1 / Heat oil in a large, heavy pot over medium heat until hot. Add leek, celery, carrot, and scallions (whites only; set aside greens to use later); season very generously with salt (about 2 teaspoons). Cook, stirring often, until vegetables have softened, about 10 minutes. Add turnip, cabbage, sorghum, and 8 cups (2 quarts) water; season very generously with salt (about 2 teaspoons). Cover and bring to a boil.

2 / Lower heat to slowly simmer soup, uncovered and stirring occasionally, until sorghum is tender, about 1 hour. Stir in asparagus. Raise heat to quickly simmer soup, uncovered and stirring occasionally, until asparagus is crisp, bright green, and tender, about 2 minutes. Finely grate zest of lemon over soup (about 1 teaspoon); squeeze juice into soup (about 2 tablespoons). Stir in reserved scallion greens, dill, and chervil (if using). Season soup with additional salt to taste.

a new victory garden—
asparagus spears
breaking ground

Spring Minestrone

————————

Spring Minestrone

Never had radishes in a soup before? You've been missing out: They offer a tender kind of comfort, like an introverted potato.

Makes about 10 bowlfuls (or 2½ quarts)

3 Meyer lemons
Kosher salt
1 bunch radishes with greens (about 10), thoroughly washed
1 large bunch ramps, spring onions, or scallions (about 6 ounces)
¼ cup olive oil
1 medium onion, chopped
2 celery stalks, chopped
1 medium carrot, peeled and chopped
1 large bunch dandelion greens, leaves thickly sliced (4 cups) and stems roughly chopped (about 1 cup)
1 cup dried pink or pinto beans, soaked overnight
6 sprigs thyme
½ cup risoni or orzo pasta (gluten-free or traditional)
1 tablespoon agave nectar, plus more to taste

1 / Finely grate zest from lemons; halve and squeeze juice from fruit. (You should have about 1 tablespoon zest and 3 tablespoons juice.) Combine lemon zest and 1 tablespoon salt in a mortar; use a pestle to smash and grind salt and zest together until it forms yellowish grit. (Alternatively, add salt to pile of lemon zest on a cutting board; chop and use side of knife to smash salt and zest together.) Halve radish bulbs and finely chop greens. Separate ramp greens from bulbs; chop separately. (You should have at least ½ cup firmly packed whites and 1 to 2 cups firmly packed greens.)

2 / Heat oil in a large, heavy pot over medium heat until hot. Add onion, celery, carrot, ramps (whites only), and half reserved Meyer lemon salt. Cook, stirring often, until vegetables have softened, about 10 minutes. Add dandelion greens, beans, thyme, radish bulbs, and 8 cups (2 quarts) water; season generously with salt (about 1 teaspoon). Cover and bring to a boil.

3 / Lower heat to slowly simmer soup, uncovered and stirring occasionally, until beans are tender, about 1 hour. Remove from heat; stir in pasta, reserved radish and ramp greens, and remaining Meyer lemon salt. Let stand, covered, until pasta and greens are softened, about 20 minutes. Stir in agave and 2 tablespoons lemon juice. Season soup with additional salt, lemon juice, and agave to taste. Remove thyme sprigs before serving.

spring supper
dappled sunlight
filling my bowl

Alabama Summer Garden Soup

Alabama Summer Garden Soup

Warning: Serve this over a bowl of grits or alongside cornbread and the lyrics of a certain Lynyrd Skynyrd anthem will just spill from your mouth.

Makes about 8 bowlfuls (or 3 quarts)

¼ cup olive oil
1 large sweet or yellow onion, chopped
2 carrots, peeled and chopped
2 celery stalks, chopped
1 red bell pepper, chopped
1 clove garlic, finely chopped
Kosher salt and freshly ground black pepper
1 pound ripe Roma tomatoes (about 6), halved
    lengthwise
1 cup dried pigeon peas (soaked for 36 hours) or
    black-eyed peas (soaked overnight)
1 small bunch mustard greens, ribs and stems removed,
    roughly torn (about 4 cups)
2 medium yellow squash (about 1 pound), halved
    lengthwise and sliced into ½-inch crescents
4 ounces fresh okra (about 6), cut into 1-inch pieces
½ teaspoon Tabasco or pepper vinegar sauce, plus more
    to taste
1 teaspoon cider vinegar, plus more to taste

1 / Heat oil in a large, heavy pot over medium heat until hot. Add onion, carrots, celery, bell pepper, and garlic; season generously with salt and pepper (about 1 teaspoon salt and ½ teaspoon pepper). Cook, stirring often, until vegetables have softened, about 10 minutes. While vegetables cook, coarsely grate cut-side of tomatoes; set pulp aside and compost tomato skins. (You should have about 1½ cups tomato pulp.) Stir in pigeon peas, mustard greens, and 8 cups (2 quarts) water; season very generously with salt (about 2 teaspoons). Cover and bring to a boil.

2 / Lower heat to slowly simmer soup, uncovered and stirring occasionally, until beans are just tender, about 1 hour. Stir in squash, okra, and reserved tomato pulp. Raise heat to quickly simmer soup, uncovered and stirring occasionally, until squash and okra are just cooked through, about 5 minutes. Stir in Tabasco and vinegar. Season soup with additional salt, Tabasco, and vinegar to taste.

Sweet Home Alabama
pigeon peas
and mustard greens

Farmer's Market Pistou

Farmer's Market Pistou

Ask the farmer if they have any tomato "seconds," which will work great in this soup and save you some cash.

Makes about 10 bowlfuls (or 3 quarts)

---

4 carrots with greens (about ½ bunch)
4 sheets dried lasagna noodles (gluten-free or traditional)
2 large heirloom tomatoes, cored and quartered
1 clove garlic, peeled
Kosher salt and freshly ground black pepper
¼ cup olive oil
1 sweet onion, chopped
2 celery stalks, chopped
4 ounces wax beans, sliced into 1-inch pieces
4 ounces green beans, sliced into 1-inch pieces
1 cup dried Great Northern beans, soaked overnight
1 bay leaf, fresh or dried
4 sprigs thyme
1 pound summer squash, such as yellow, pattypan, or zucchini, cut into 1-inch pieces
½ cup Vegan Pesto (page 164) or store-bought for serving

1 / Peel and chop carrots. Wash, dry, and finely chop carrot greens (leafy fronds only; compost long stalks). (You should have about ½ cup chopped carrot greens.) Snap noodles into approximately 2-inch pieces. In a blender jar, combine tomatoes, garlic, and 1 teaspoon salt; blend until smooth. Place blender jar next to stove.

2 / Heat oil in a large, heavy pot over medium heat until hot. Add onion, celery, and carrots (roots only); season generously with salt and pepper (about 1 teaspoon salt and ½ teaspoon pepper). Cook, stirring often, until vegetables have softened, about 10 minutes. Add wax and green beans, soaked beans, bay leaf, thyme, reserved carrot tops, reserved tomato purée, and 8 cups (2 quarts) water; season generously with salt (about 1 teaspoon). Cover and bring to a boil.

3 / Lower heat to slowly simmer soup, covered and without stirring, until beans are tender, about 1½ hours. Remove from heat; stir in broken noodles and squash. Let stand, covered, until pasta and squash have softened, about 20 minutes. Season soup with additional salt to taste. Serve soup topped with a spoonful of pesto (or stir full amount into pot before serving). Remove bay leaf and thyme sprigs before serving.

soup mug
savoring the broth
on my chin

Summer Succotash Soup

Summer Succotash Soup

Slice fresh kernels from two corn cobs (about 1½ cups total) and stir them into the soup at the end of cooking.

Makes about 8 bowlfuls (or 4 quarts)

½ cup olive oil
1 large sweet onion, chopped
1 large green bell pepper, chopped
3 large red, yellow, or orange bell peppers, chopped
2 cloves garlic, chopped
Kosher salt
2 tablespoons yellow or brown mustard seeds
1 tablespoon smoked paprika
¼ teaspoon red pepper flakes
4 sprigs fresh thyme
1 pound dried black-eyed peas, soaked overnight
1½ pounds unripe, green tomatoes or tomatillos, husk removed, roughly chopped
½ cup basil leaves (from 1 bunch), roughly torn
Cornbread for serving

1 / Heat oil in a large, heavy pot over medium heat until hot; add onion, bell peppers, and garlic. Season generously with salt (about 1 teaspoon). Cook, stirring often, until peppers are soft and their juices have reduced and thickened to a sweet syrup, about 15 minutes. Stir in mustard seeds, paprika, pepper flakes, thyme, beans, tomatoes, and 6 cups (1½ quarts) water. Season generously with salt (about 2 teaspoons). Cover and bring to a boil. Lower heat and simmer soup, covered, until beans are tender but haven't yet begun to break apart, about 40 minutes. Stir in basil. Season soup with additional salt to taste. Remove thyme stems before serving.

summer succotash—
seeing old friends
renewed again

15-Bean Soup

15-Bean Soup

Use up remnant bags of beans for this soup or help one of those weird, random bags of mixed beans from the store fulfill their culinary destiny.

Makes about 8 bowlfuls (or 2½ quarts)

¼ cup nutritional yeast
4 dried bay leaves, crumbled
½ teaspoon celery seed
1 tablespoon smoked paprika
2 teaspoons chili powder
¼ cup olive oil
1 large onion, chopped
1 large green bell pepper, chopped
4 garlic cloves, chopped
Kosher salt and freshly ground black pepper
1½ pounds (20 ounces) mixed dried beans (or 20-ounce bag 15-Bean Soup®, seasoning packet discarded), soaked overnight
1 (14.5-ounce) can diced tomatoes
1 tablespoon cider vinegar, plus more to taste

1 / In a spice grinder, combine yeast, bay leaves, and celery seed; process until finely ground. In a small bowl, stir together ground spices with paprika and chili powder. Set aside.

2 / Heat oil in a large, heavy pot over medium heat until hot; add onion, bell pepper, and garlic. Season generously with salt and pepper (about 1 teaspoon salt and ½ teaspoon pepper). Cook, stirring often, until vegetables have softened, about 8 minutes. Stir in beans, tomatoes, reserved spice mixture, and 6 cups (1½ quarts) water. Season generously with salt (about 2 teaspoons). Cover and bring to a boil.

3 / Lower heat and simmer soup, uncovered, until beans are tender, about 1 hour. Raise heat to quickly simmer soup, stirring occasionally, until broth has reduced to a thick, flavorful gravy, about 15 minutes. Stir in vinegar. Season soup with additional salt and vinegar to taste.

15 bean soup
so many ways
to say I love you

Skillet Supper Bread

Skillet Supper Bread

For those who had a bad breakup with cornbread, I offer its gentler twin to swoon over.

Makes 1 (8 or 9-inch) round loaf

---

2 cups millet or coarse cornmeal
¼ cup flax seed
1 tablespoon nutritional yeast
1 teaspoon baking soda
1 teaspoon paprika
1 teaspoon Kosher salt
2 tablespoons butter, preferably salted and grass-fed
2 large eggs
1½ cups buttermilk
1 tablespoon honey

1 / Preheat oven to 400°F. In a blender jar, combine millet, flax seed, yeast, baking soda, paprika, and salt. Blend until millet is about halfway ground, about 1 minute. (Test this by stopping the blender and rubbing some of the mixture between your fingers; it should feel coarse but your fingers should be powdery.)

2 / Add butter to an 8 or 9-inch cast-iron skillet; transfer skillet to hot oven for pan to preheat 5 minutes. Meanwhile, in a large bowl, whisk together eggs, buttermilk, and honey until fully combined. Add dry ingredients and stir to form a thick batter. Carefully scrape batter into prepared pan; smooth the top.

3 / Return skillet to the oven; bake bread until golden around the edges and a skewer inserted in the center tests clean, about 25 minutes.

VEGAN VARIATION: Substitute 1½ cups almond milk plus 1 teaspoon cider vinegar for buttermilk; avocado oil for butter; agave nectar for honey. Omit eggs.

suppertime
lifting the day's weight
my cast-iron skillet

Favorite Yeast Roll

Favorite Yeast Roll

These rolls are already gluten-free and vegan but can be made grain free, or even with traditional wheat all-purpose flour. If these rolls were sideshow talent performers, they would merit a show in Vegas for their quick-change artistry.

Makes 1 dozen

¼ cup flax seed (40 grams)
1 cup (128 grams) tapioca flour
1 cup (124 grams) sorghum flour
1 cup (132 grams) brown rice flour
½ teaspoon (2 grams) xanthan gum
1 teaspoon (3 grams) Kosher salt
1 tablespoon nigella seeds (sometimes called "kalongi," "black cumin,"
   or "black caraway"), plus more for sprinkling, optional
1¼ cups warm water (105°F to 110°F)
2 tablespoons maple syrup
1 (¼-ounce) package active dry yeast
¼ cup olive oil, plus more for brushing
Softened vegan butter or non-hydrogenated vegetable oil for tin

1 / Grind flax seed in a spice grinder until finely ground. Whisk together flours, xanthan gum, salt, and nigella seeds (if using) in a medium bowl. In the bowl of an electric mixer, combine water, maple syrup, ground flax, and yeast; let stand 5 minutes. (Mixture will puff and become foamy.) Add oil and flour to liquid. Brush cups of a 12-cup muffin tin with softened butter or non-hydrogenated vegetable oil.

2 / Using a stand mixer fitted with a paddle attachment (or wooden spoon and elbow grease), mix dough for 5 minutes on medium speed. (Dough will become sticky and smooth.) Use an oiled ¼-cup dry measuring cup to scoop dough into prepared muffin cups. Sprinkle dough portions with nigella seeds, if desired.

3 / Cover dish loosely with a clean kitchen towel and set in a warm, draft-free spot until the rolls are doubled in volume, about 1 hour. Preheat oven to 400°F.

4 / Bake rolls until they are evenly golden brown, about 40 minutes. Transfer muffin tin to a wire rack until rolls are cool enough to release from muffin tin, about 10 minutes. Cool rolls completely on wire rack before serving.

TRADITIONAL VARIATION: Swap 3 cups all-purpose flour (spooned and leveled) for tapioca, sorghum, and brown rice flours. Omit xanthan gum.

GRAIN-FREE VARIATION: Swap 3 cups Homemade Grain-Free Flour Blend (page 165) for tapioca, sorghum, and brown rice flours.

full moon
rising at day's end
warm dinner rolls

Flaky Buttermilk Biscuit

Flaky Buttermilk Biscuit

Make these biscuits extra fancy by sprinkling in chopped rosemary or thyme leaves as you roll and fold the dough.

Makes 1 dozen

2 cups all-purpose flour (traditional or gluten-free, or use Homemade Grain-Free Flour Blend on page 165), plus more for surface
¼ cup blanched almond flour
1 teaspoon xanthan gum
1 tablespoon baking powder
1 teaspoon baking soda
½ teaspoon Kosher salt
1½ sticks unsalted butter, frozen
1 cup buttermilk, cold, plus more for brushing

1 / Whisk together all-purpose flour, almond flour, xanthan, baking powder, baking soda, and salt in a baking dish or shallow bowl. Place a box grater in center of dish; coarsely grate butter directly into flour mixture.

2 / Working quickly, toss grated butter pieces with flour to separate. Drizzle buttermilk over flour mixture and use a fork to combine dough. Turn dough out onto a large piece of plastic wrap; use wrap to gather and form dough into an approximate 6-inch square. (Dough will be lumpy and slightly wet.) Wrap dough tightly in plastic wrap and chill until firm, about 30 minutes.

3 / Dust a parchment-lined work surface with flour. Use a floured pin to roll dough into a rectangle about the size of a piece of paper with the short side nearest you. Fold the dough as if fitting into an envelope: the lower third folds up onto itself, the upper third folds on top of that. Re-wrap dough and chill until firm. Repeat this step twice, alternating the direction of the folds.

4 / Preheat oven to 400°F with racks dividing oven into upper and lower thirds. Line a baking sheet with parchment or a Silpat. Unwrap and return dough to parchment-lined, floured surface. Roll dough into a 1-inch-thick patty. Using a floured 2-inch cutter, cut chilled dough into rounds. (Swiftly press and gather scraps together to re-form patty.) Arrange dough rounds on prepared baking sheet about 2 inches apart. (All 12 will fit on the sheet.) Place baking sheet in the refrigerator until disks are solid, about 20 minutes.

5 / Brush chilled disks with buttermilk. Transfer baking sheets to oven. Bake, swapping and rotating sheets after 10 minutes, until biscuits are puffed and golden brown, about 15 minutes. Remove biscuits to a wire rack to cool completely.

VEGAN VERSION: Swap vegan butter for butter and almond or coconut yogurt for buttermilk.

snowfall
melting flakes on my tongue
buttermilk biscuits

The Cookie

The Cookie

These cookies are their own language of love——share them wisely.

Makes about 4 dozen cookies

3¼ cups (445 grams) all-purpose flour, spooned and leveled
¼ cup (35 grams) cornstarch
1¼ teaspoons (5 grams) baking powder
1 rounded teaspoon (7 grams) Kosher salt, plus more for sprinkling
1 teaspoon (6 grams) baking soda
2 sticks (8 ounces) unsalted butter, at room temperature
1 cup (212 grams) granulated sugar
1 packed cup (200 grams) light brown sugar
2 large eggs, at room temperature
2 teaspoons pure vanilla extract
1 pound best-quality bittersweet chocolate (50–75% cacao content), chopped (about 3½ cups)

1 / Whisk together dry ingredients in a medium bowl: flour, cornstarch, baking powder, salt, and baking soda; set aside. In the bowl of an electric mixer, beat butter with sugars until very light and fluffy, doubled in volume, and no longer sandy to the touch, pausing to scrape down the sides of the bowl once, about 4 minutes. With mixer on medium speed, beat in eggs one at a time until combined; add vanilla. With the mixer on low, add flour mixture a heaping spoonful at a time, pausing to let each one incorporate. Stir in chopped chocolate by hand.

2 / Use a 1-ounce cookie scoop (or a slightly heaping tablespoon measure) to scoop portions of dough into about 1½-inch balls onto a parchment-lined baking sheet (they can touch). Repeat with remaining dough. Cover baking sheet with waxed paper or plastic wrap and chill 1 hour. (The baking sheet can also be transferred to the freezer at this point; once the dough portions are frozen, they can be broken apart and transferred to a zip-top freezer bag, stored up to 3 months, and baked directly from frozen.)

3 / To bake, preheat oven to 350°F with racks dividing the oven into upper and lower thirds. Arrange dough portions onto parchment- or Silpat-lined baking sheets a few inches apart (12 per sheet). Sprinkle cookies with additional Kosher salt. Bake cookies, rotating pans halfway through, until no longer wet-looking and very lightly golden brown around edges, 12 to 14 minutes. Rest cookies on baking sheets 5 minutes; use a thin spatula to transfer cookies to wire racks to cool completely.

Cookie Variations on page 126

salted chocolate
impossible to bite off
more than I can chew

Cookie Variations

Here is the extent of my secrets, guys.
My favorite brands of chocolate are Guittard, Ghiradelli, Valrhona, and the Belgian chocolate they sell at Trader Joe's. The secret isn't which chocolate you use, as long as it's high quality (one you would choose to eat alone, not just bake with). I prefer to use a mix of two dark chocolates with different cacao contents for layered flavor. Chips just don't cut it, I hate to say. I make these cookies in very large quantities, so I prefer to measure in grams, in favor of speed and accuracy. You do you.

Electric Mixer Variation
Decrease flour to 3 cups (415 grams) and cornstarch to 2 tablespoons (otherwise keep ingredient list the same). Whisk together dry ingredients in a medium bowl: flour, cornstarch, baking powder, salt, and baking soda; set aside. Place butter in a large bowl. Using a handheld electric mixer fitted with double beaters, beat butter until smooth and light (about 1 minute). Add brown and white sugars. Beat sugars and butter together on mixer's highest setting, pausing to scrape the sides of the bowl once, until very light, fluffy, and spreadable, like frosting (about 10 minutes). Beat in eggs one at a time, then vanilla, until incorporated. Beat on highest setting, pausing to scrape the sides of the bowl once, until doubled in volume (about 3 minutes). Working by hand, stir in flour mixture in 3 additions until just combined; stir in chocolate. Resume with step 2 in method above. Makes about 40 cookies.

Vegan Variation
Make vegan eggs by combining 2 tablespoons golden flaxseeds and ¼ teaspoon baking powder in a spice grinder and grind to a fine powder; transfer to a bowl with ½ cup warm water. Stir and set aside 10 minutes (it will be wobbly, firm, and cool to the touch when ready). Swap in vegan chocolate (my pick: the Seattle local favorite, Theo, of course!) and cultured vegan butter or non-hydrogenated vegetable shortening. Follow the method above for step 2. Decrease baking time to 8 to 10 minutes and cool cookies on cookie sheets 2 minutes before removing to a wire rack to cool completely.

Gluten-Free (and Grain-Free!) Variation
Substitute favorite all-purpose gluten-free flour mixture for the all-purpose flour in traditional recipe, or make mine on page 165.

Chopped Winter Salad

Chopped Winter Salad

Outturn the pockets of your cabinets for this salad, tossing in handfuls of nuts and dried fruit. Use leftover inner stalks of celery from making soup.

Serves 4

---

2 blood oranges
2 tablespoons cider vinegar
1 tablespoon agave nectar
1 small Belgian endive (about 5 ounces)
½ small head radicchio (about 6 ounces) or Treviso
1 celery heart (pale green inner stalks of celery with leaves)
1 head gem lettuce (about 3 ounces) or ½ small head romaine
¼ cup dried fruit (my pick would be currants)
¼ cup toasted seeds or nuts (like pumpkin or pistachio)
¼ cup olive oil, divided
Kosher salt and freshly ground black pepper
1 slice (1-ounce) gluten-free sandwich bread, coarsely grated (about
  ½ cup crumbs)

1 / Cut oranges in half horizontally, along their middle. Slice topmost stem edge of one half of orange away, exposing fruit. Cut peel away in strips, running knife along the curve of the fruit from one end of exposed fruit to the other. (Bits of pith may remain.) Cut peeled half of orange into quarters. Remove peel of both halves of the second orange. (You should have three orange halves without their peel, each cut into quarters, and one with a peel intact.) Heat a medium, heavy skillet (such as cast-iron) over high heat (do not add oil). Add unpeeled orange half, cut-side down, to skillet. Sear until fruit is charred in spots, about 3 minutes. Remove pan from heat. Add vinegar and agave to skillet (it will sizzle), scraping up blackened bits as it boils. Scrape vinegar mixture into a liquid measuring cup; set aside. Rinse, dry, and reserve skillet.

2 / Add 1 tablespoon oil in reserved skillet over medium heat until hot. Add bread crumbs; season generously with salt and pepper (about ½ teaspoon salt and ¼ teaspoon pepper). Cook, stirring often, until bread crumbs are a dark golden brown, about 5 minutes.

3 / Chop endive, radicchio, celery heart, and gem lettuce into 1 to 1½-inch pieces; transfer greens into a large serving bowl. Add reserved quartered orange, dried fruit, and nuts/seeds. Squeeze juice from charred blood orange half into reserved vinegar mixture. (You should have around 2 tablespoons charred juice.) Add remaining oil; season generously with salt and pepper (about ½ teaspoon salt and ¼ teaspoon pepper). Stir dressing together until it becomes cloudy; pour over salad. Use clean hands to scoop underneath the greens to gently "toss" a few times, pausing once to season greens with salt and pepper. Scatter tossed salad with bread crumbs and bring to the table with a large spoon for serving.

midwinter break
a burst of sunshine
blood oranges

Spring Arrival Salad

Spring Arrival Salad

This salad is all about tender greens and herbs mixed with crunchy, lightly pickled veggies and a creamy dressing. Add feta or roasted new potatoes to the mix for next-level spring comfort.

Serves 4

1 small bunch (about 6) radishes, scrubbed and quartered (about 1 cup), greens composted
2 medium carrots, peeled, halved lengthwise, and sliced into 1-inch pieces (about 1 cup)
½ small red onion, peeled, halved, and sliced about ¼ inch thick
1 cup cider vinegar
Kosher salt and freshly ground black pepper
1 bunch parsley, leaves stripped from stems, stems roughly chopped (about ½ cup)
1 bunch chives, snipped into 1-inch pieces
2 cups baby arugula (about ½ 5-ounce container)
2 cups baby spinach (about ½ 5-ounce container)
4 ounces (about 1 cup) sugar snap peas, sliced ¼ inch thick (about ½ cup)
¼ cup tahini
2 tablespoons freshly squeezed lemon juice, plus more to taste
¼ cup olive oil
2 teaspoons toasted sesame oil
Sesame seeds for sprinkling, optional

1 / Combine radishes, carrots, and red onion in a medium saucepan. Add cider vinegar and 1 cup water to saucepan with the vegetables; season very generously with salt and pepper (about 2 teaspoons salt and ½ teaspoon pepper). Bring to a boil. Remove saucepan from heat, cover, and set aside 10 minutes. Use a slotted spoon to lift pickled vegetables from brine and transfer to a bowl of ice water.

2 / Place parsley stems in a blender jar with half of the chives (about ¼ cup); set aside. Combine parsley leaves in a large salad bowl with remaining chives, arugula, spinach, and snap peas.

3 / Add tahini, lemon juice, and ¼ cup water (or enough to loosen mixture enough for blade to run smoothly) to blender jar with herbs; season very generously with salt and pepper (about 2 teaspoons salt and ½ teaspoon pepper). With motor running, drizzle in olive oil. Season dressing with more lemon juice, salt, and pepper to taste.

4 / Drain pickled vegetables well and pat dry; add to greens in bowl. Drizzle greens and pickled vegetables with sesame oil. Use clean hands to scoop underneath the greens, lifting them through the vegetables and wiggling your fingers to gently "toss" a few times, pausing once to season greens with salt and pepper. (Salad ingredients will be jumbled together with pickled vegetables.) Arrange salad on a platter and spoon herb dressing over top; scatter salad with sesame seeds, if desired. Bring salad to the table with a large spoon for serving.

bright pink radishes
emerging from winter
to hope again

Instant Pot Variations

Brush off that gift your mom picked up for you at Costco; it won't bite. Let this section help you make soups in an instant—without the need to soak beans, either. (For more on beans, see "All About Beans" on page xi.) These recipes are written as speedier versions of their glamorous stovetop counterparts throughout the pages of this book. Reference your model's manual for valve release instructions and pick the method that makes you comfortable. Want Caroline's advice? Be brave, stand back, and let the steam fly.

Mexican Butter Bean Soup

1 large onion, quartered

1 (14.5-ounce) can diced tomatoes

4 cloves garlic, peeled

¼ teaspoon saffron threads

½ cup avocado oil

1 teaspoon ground cumin

1 teaspoon ground coriander

Kosher salt and freshly ground black pepper

1 pound dried butter beans (see note on page xi)

1 lime

In a blender jar, combine onion and tomatoes; blend until smooth and set aside. Chop garlic and saffron threads together until golden and finely chopped. Set Instant Pot to SAUTÉ, and follow manufacturer's instructions to select middle temperature setting (NORMAL). Heat oil in metal insert until prompt indicates HOT. Add chopped garlic mixture, cumin, and coriander. Cook, stirring constantly, until spices are fragrant, about 30 seconds. Stir in reserved onion purée; season generously with salt and pepper (about 1 teaspoon salt and ½ teaspoon pepper). Cook until sauce thickens and turns bright orange, about 5 minutes. Press CANCEL. Add beans and 4 cups (1 quart) water; season very generously with salt (about 2 teaspoons). Close and lock the lid; seal valve (set to SEALING). Set to PRESSURE COOK with setting on HIGH. Set time to 25 minutes. When timer rings, press CANCEL; follow manufacturer's instructions to release pressure. Finely grate 1 teaspoon zest from lime, and squeeze from it 1 tablespoon juice; stir both into soup. Season soup with additional salt and lime juice to taste.

Ribollita

¼ cup olive oil

1 medium onion, chopped

2 celery stalks, chopped

1 medium carrot, peeled and chopped

Kosher salt and freshly ground black pepper

2 medium potatoes, sweet or regular, peeled and cut into 2-inch chunks

1 small bunch broccoli rabe, cut into 1-inch pieces

1 small bunch kale, ribs and stems removed, thinly sliced

1 cup dried Great Northern beans (see note on page xi)

4 sprigs thyme

1 (14.5-oz) can diced tomatoes

1 teaspoon freshly squeezed lemon juice, plus more to taste

Set Instant Pot to SAUTÉ, and follow manufacturer's instructions to select middle temperature setting (NORMAL). Heat oil in metal insert until prompt indicates HOT, and add onion, celery, and carrot; season generously with salt and pepper (about 1 teaspoon salt and ½ teaspoon pepper). Cook, stirring often, until vegetables have softened, about 10 minutes. Stir in potato, broccoli rabe, kale, beans, thyme, tomatoes, and 6 cups (1½ quarts) water. Season very generously with salt (about 2 teaspoons). Press CANCEL. Close and lock the lid; seal valve (set to SEALING). Set to PRESSURE COOK with setting on HIGH. Set time to 25 minutes. When timer rings, press CANCEL; follow manufacturer's instructions to release pressure. Stir in lemon juice. Season soup with additional salt and lemon juice to taste. Remove thyme sprigs before serving.

Cowboy Chili

¼ cup ground chicory or decaf coffee

2 tablespoons molasses

1 large onion, chopped

1 large green bell pepper, chopped

Kosher salt

¼ cup avocado oil

4 cloves garlic, chopped

¼ cup Toasted Chili Powder (page 163) or 2 tablespoons store-bought

¼ cup nutritional yeast

2 tablespoons unsweetened carob or cocoa powder

1 tablespoon smoked paprika

1 (28-ounce) can crushed tomatoes

1 cup dried black beans (see note on page xi)

1 cup dried small red beans (see note on page xi)

1 tablespoon cider vinegar, plus more to taste

Cornbread for serving

Stir to combine chicory, molasses, and 2 cups boiling water in a liquid measuring cup; set aside. Heat a large cast-iron skillet over high heat until very hot (do not add oil); add onion and bell pepper in a single layer. Cook, without stirring, until vegetables are charred around edges, about 8 minutes; season with salt (about 1 teaspoon). Scrape charred vegetables into metal insert. Stir in oil, garlic, chili powder, yeast, carob, paprika, tomatoes, black and red beans, and 4 cups (1 quart) water; season generously with salt (about 1 teaspoon). Strain brewed chicory mixture into pot through a fine-mesh sieve lined with cheesecloth or single sheet of damp paper towel. Close and lock the lid; seal valve (set to SEALING). Set to PRESSURE COOK with setting on HIGH. Set time to 35 minutes. When timer rings, press CANCEL; follow manufacturer's instructions to release pressure. Return pot to SAUTÉ (NORMAL). Simmer chili, stirring constantly and mashing beans to create a cloudy gravy, until it is thick, about 10 minutes. Stir in vinegar. Season chili with additional salt and vinegar to taste. Serve with cornbread.

Tomato and Quinoa Soup

1 medium onion, cut into 8 wedges with root end intact

4 cloves garlic, peeled

4 large carrots, peeled and cut into 1-inch pieces

1 teaspoon thyme leaves

¼ cup olive oil, divided

Kosher salt and freshly ground black pepper

2 tablespoons tomato paste

2 bay leaves, fresh or dried

1 cup uncooked quinoa, rinsed if desired

1 (28-ounce) can diced tomatoes

1 (28-ounce) can crushed tomatoes

3 tablespoons agave nectar, plus more to taste

1 teaspoon cider vinegar, plus more to taste

Heat broiler with rack about 5 inches away from heat. On a large rimmed baking sheet, toss onion, garlic, carrots, and thyme with 2 tablespoons oil; season generously with salt and pepper (about 1 teaspoon salt and ½ teaspoon pepper). Broil vegetables, tossing every 2 minutes, until golden brown in spots and tender when pierced, about 10 minutes. Transfer vegetables to a blender jar with 1 cup water; blend, cracking lid and covering with a towel to release steam, until smooth. Set Instant Pot to SAUTÉ, and follow manufacturer's instructions to select middle temperature setting (NORMAL). Heat remaining oil in metal insert until prompt indicates HOT. Add tomato paste (it will spatter); cook, stirring, until the oil turns red, about 2 minutes. Press CANCEL. Let stand to cool slightly, 2 minutes. Stir in vegetable purée, scraping bottom and sides of pot with wooden spoon to release any caramelized tomato. Stir in bay leaves, quinoa, and 3 cups (¾ quart) water. Pour in canned tomatoes (both diced and crushed); do not stir. Close and lock the lid; seal valve (set to SEALING). Set to PRESSURE COOK with setting on HIGH. Set time to 20 minutes. When timer rings, press CANCEL; follow manufacturer's instructions to release pressure. Stir in agave and vinegar. Season soup with additional salt, agave, and vinegar to taste. Remove bay leaves before serving.

Egyptian Chickpea and Okra Stew

½ cup olive oil

1 large onion, chopped

3 large celery stalks, chopped

1 pound fresh or frozen okra, cut into 1-inch pieces

2 cloves garlic, chopped

¼ cup nutritional yeast

1 tablespoon ground cumin

2 teaspoons ground coriander

1 pound dried chickpeas (see note on page xi)

1 (28-ounce) can crushed tomatoes

1 dried Árbol chile, optional

Kosher salt

2 tablespoons freshly squeezed lemon juice, plus more to taste

Set Instant Pot to SAUTÉ, and follow manufacturer's instructions to select middle temperature setting (NORMAL). Heat oil in metal insert until prompt indicates HOT. Add onion and celery. Cook, stirring often, until vegetables have softened, about 10 minutes. Stir in okra, garlic, yeast, cumin, coriander, chickpeas, tomatoes, chile (if using), and 5 cups (1¼ quarts) water; season very generously with salt (about 1 tablespoon). Press CANCEL. Close and lock the lid; seal valve (set to SEALING). Set to PRESSURE COOK with setting on HIGH. Set time to 35 minutes. When timer rings, press CANCEL; follow manufacturer's instructions to release pressure. Return pot to SAUTÉ (NORMAL). Simmer stew, stirring constantly to break apart the okra, until broth has reduced to a thick, flavorful gravy, about 10 minutes. Stir in lemon juice. Season stew with additional salt and lemon juice to taste. Discard chile, if used, before serving.

Parsi Squash Stew

¼ cup coconut oil

1 large onion, chopped

4 cloves garlic, finely chopped

1 (1-inch) piece fresh ginger, peeled and chopped

Kosher salt

1½ teaspoons ground turmeric

1 teaspoon ground coriander

1 teaspoon ground cumin

¼ teaspoon ground cloves

2 bay leaves, fresh or dried

1 (14.5-ounce) can diced tomatoes

½ cup dried chickpeas (see note on page xi)

½ cup dried mung beans

½ cup dried red lentils

1 delicata squash (about 1 pound), halved lengthwise, seeds scooped away and composted, and cut into 2-inch pieces (do not peel)

1 teaspoon cider vinegar, plus more to taste

4 cups baby spinach (¾ of 5-ounce container)

Set Instant Pot to SAUTÉ, and follow manufacturer's instructions to select middle temperature setting (NORMAL). Heat oil in metal insert until prompt indicates HOT. Add onion, garlic, and ginger; season generously with salt (about 1 teaspoon). Cook, stirring often, until vegetables have softened and are starting to brown, about 5 minutes. Stir in turmeric, coriander, cumin, cloves, bay leaves, tomatoes, chickpeas, mung beans, lentils, squash, and 6 cups (1½ quarts) water; season very generously with salt (about 2 teaspoons). Press CANCEL. Close and lock the lid; seal valve (set to SEALING). Set to PRESSURE COOK with setting on HIGH. Set time to 25 minutes. When timer rings, press CANCEL; follow manufacturer's instructions to release pressure. Add vinegar. Stir in spinach by the handful. Season stew with additional salt and vinegar to taste. Remove bay leaves before serving.

Pumpkin-Coconut Soup with Curry Leaves

6 cloves garlic, peeled

1 (1-inch) piece fresh ginger, peeled and sliced

1 large onion, peeled and quartered

¼ cup coconut oil

¼ cup firmly packed curry leaves, fresh or dried

2 tablespoons Homemade Curry Powder (page 162) or store-bought

1 (15-ounce) can pure pumpkin purée

1 small kabocha squash (about 2 pounds), peeled, seeds removed, and cut into very large (3-inch) chunks

4 cups cubed, peeled butternut squash (from 1 small)

2 small sweet potatoes or yams, peeled and cut into 2-inch pieces

Kosher salt

2 cups full-fat coconut cream (from a well-shaken carton, such as Aroy-D brand; sold in Asian markets)

1 teaspoon Homemade Garam Masala (page 162) or store-bought

2 tablespoons freshly squeezed lemon juice, plus more to taste

Pumpkin seeds for serving, optional

In a blender jar, combine garlic, ginger, onion, and ¼ cup water; blend until smooth and set aside. Set Instant Pot to SAUTÉ, and follow manufacturer's instructions to select middle temperature setting (NORMAL). Heat oil in metal insert until prompt indicates HOT. Add curry leaves and cook until crisp and fragrant, about 1 minute. (They won't brown.) Stir in curry powder, pumpkin purée, reserved blended onion mixture, and 4 cups (1 quart) water until combined. Add squash (both kabocha and butternut) and sweet potatoes. Season very generously with salt (about 2 teaspoons). Press CANCEL. Close and lock the lid; seal valve (set to SEALING). Set to PRESSURE COOK with setting on HIGH. Set time to 8 minutes. When timer rings, press CANCEL; follow manufacturer's instructions to release pressure. Stir in coconut cream and garam masala. Return pot to SAUTÉ (NORMAL). Simmer soup, stirring often to break apart potatoes and create a rich gravy, until it is thick, about 5 minutes. Stir in lemon juice. Season soup with additional salt and lemon juice to taste. Serve soup topped with pumpkin seeds, if desired.

Morroccan Vegetable Stew

1 small bunch cilantro (about 10 sprigs)

1 small bunch parsley (about 10 sprigs)

¼ cup firmly packed mint leaves (stripped from about 4 sprigs), finely chopped

½ cup olive oil

1 large onion, chopped

2 cloves garlic, chopped

1 (1-inch) piece fresh ginger, peeled and chopped

Kosher salt

½ cup Homemade Harissa (page 163) or 2 tablespoons store-bought

2 teaspoons ground cumin

1 teaspoon dried turmeric

2 strips orange zest, peeled with a vegetable peeler and thinly sliced

1 (28-ounce) can diced tomatoes

1 cup dried chickpeas (see note on page xi)

1 large sweet potato, peeled and quartered

3 large carrots, peeled and cut into 2-inch chunks

½ medium head cauliflower, cored and cut into bite-sized florets (about 3 cups)

2 medium zucchini, quartered lengthwise and sliced into ¾-inch chunks

1 tablespoon freshly squeezed lemon juice, plus more to taste

Separate cilantro leaves from stems; finely chop both, separately. Repeat with parsley; place herb stems in one bowl and leaves in another, combining cilantro, parsley, and mint. (You should have 1 firmly packed tablespoon combined stems and ½ firmly packed cup combined leaves; set aside.) Set Instant Pot to SAUTÉ, and follow manufacturer's instructions to select middle temperature setting (NORMAL). Heat oil in metal insert until prompt indicates HOT. Add onion, garlic, and ginger; season generously with salt (about 1 teaspoon). Cook, stirring often, until vegetables are beginning to soften but not browned, about 5 minutes. Stir in harissa, cumin, turmeric, zest, tomatoes, chickpeas, potato, carrot, and 4 cups (1 quart) water; season very generously with salt (about 2 teaspoons). Press CANCEL. Close and lock the lid; seal valve (set to SEALING). Set to PRESSURE COOK with setting on HIGH. Set time to 30 minutes. When timer rings, press CANCEL; follow manufacturer's instructions to release pressure. Add cauliflower and zucchini. Return pot to SAUTÉ (NORMAL). Simmer stew, stirring occasionally, until cauliflower and zucchini are tender, about 8 minutes. Stir in lemon juice and remaining reserved chopped herbs. Season stew with additional salt and lemon juice to taste.

Split Pea Soup with Roasted Kale

1 medium bunch kale (curly preferred), trimmed of thick stems and ribs and chopped (about 6 packed cups)

2 tablespoons + ½ cup olive oil, divided

Kosher salt and freshly ground black pepper

6 cloves garlic, peeled, smashed with knife

1 medium onion, chopped

2 celery stalks, chopped

2 medium carrots, peeled and sliced into ½-inch-thick disks

2 tablespoons mustard seeds or 1 tablespoon ground mustard

¼ cup nutritional yeast

2 teaspoons smoked paprika

2 bay leaves, fresh or dried

⅛ teaspoon freshly grated nutmeg

1 pound dried green or yellow split peas (see note on page xi)

2 teaspoons cider vinegar, plus more to taste

Heat broiler with rack about 5 inches from heat. On a large rimmed baking sheet, toss kale with 2 tablespoons oil and season generously with salt and pepper (about 1 teaspoon salt and ½ teaspoon pepper); scrunch and squeeze greens until soft. Broil greens, tossing every 2 minutes, until charred at the edges, about 6 minutes. (You should have about 2 cups roasted kale.) Set Instant Pot to SAUTÉ, or follow manufacturer's instructions to select middle temperature setting (NORMAL). Heat remaining oil in metal insert until prompt indicates HOT. Add garlic, onion, celery, and carrots; season generously with salt and pepper (about 1 teaspoon salt and ½ teaspoon pepper). Cook, stirring often, until vegetables have softened, about 10 minutes. Add mustard seeds, yeast, paprika, bay leaves, and nutmeg; cook, stirring often, until spices are fragrant, about 2 minutes. Stir in split peas, reserved roasted kale, and 7 cups (1¾ quarts) water; season generously with salt (about 1 teaspoon). Press CANCEL. Close and lock the lid; seal valve (set to SEALING). Set to PRESSURE COOK with setting on HIGH. Set time to 12 minutes. When timer rings, press CANCEL; follow manufacturer's instructions to release pressure. Stir in vinegar. Season soup to taste with additional salt and vinegar. Remove bay leaves before serving.

White Bean Chili with Tomatillo

¼ cup avocado oil

1 large onion, chopped

1 large green bell pepper, chopped

Kosher salt

6 cloves garlic, chopped

2 tablespoons Green Chili Powder (page 163)

1½ pounds tomatillos (about 12), husk removed and roughly chopped

1 pound dried Great Northern beans (see note on page xi)

2 firmly packed tablespoons chopped cilantro leaves

Set Instant Pot to SAUTÉ, and follow manufacturer's instructions to select middle temperature setting (NORMAL). Heat oil in metal insert until prompt indicates HOT. Add onion and bell pepper; season generously with salt (about 1 teaspoon). Cook, stirring often, until vegetables have softened, about 10 minutes. Stir in garlic, chili powder, tomatillos, beans, and 5 cups (1¼ quarts) water; season very generously with salt (about 2 teaspoons). Press CANCEL. Close and lock the lid; seal valve (set to SEALING). Set to PRESSURE COOK with setting on HIGH. Set time to 35 minutes. When timer rings, press CANCEL; follow manufacturer's instructions to release pressure. Return pot to SAUTÉ (NORMAL). Simmer chili, stirring constantly and mashing beans to create a cloudy gravy, until it is thick, about 10 minutes. Stir in cilantro. Season chili with additional salt to taste.

Catalan Chickpea Stew with Spinach

¾ cup olive oil

6 cloves garlic, peeled

½ cup parsley leaves, well-dried

¼ cup pine nuts

1 (1-ounce) slice gluten-free sandwich bread, coarsely grated (about ½ cup crumbs)

1 large onion, chopped

Kosher salt and freshly ground black pepper

¼ cup tomato paste

1 tablespoon smoked paprika

1 pound dried chickpeas (see note on page xi)

½ cup currants

2 teaspoons sherry or cider vinegar, plus more to taste

5 cups baby spinach (5-ounce container)

Set Instant Pot to SAUTÉ, and follow manufacturer's instructions to select middle temperature setting (NORMAL). Heat oil in metal insert until prompt indicates HOT. Add garlic, parsley, pine nuts, and bread crumbs. Cook, stirring, until pine nuts and bread crumbs are a deep golden brown, about 5 minutes. Use a slotted spoon to remove ingredients to a bowl, reserving oil. Add onion; cook, stirring often, until onion has softened, about 10 minutes. While onion cooks, transfer reserved bread crumb mixture to a food processor, season generously with salt and pepper (about 1 teaspoon salt and ½ teaspoon pepper), and blend until smooth to make a picada; set aside. Stir tomato paste, paprika, and reserved picada into onions. Add chickpeas and 5 cups (1¼ quarts) water; season very generously with salt (about 2 teaspoons). Press CANCEL. Close and lock the lid; seal valve (set to SEALING). Set to PRESSURE COOK with setting on HIGH. Set time to 35 minutes. When timer rings, press CANCEL; follow manufacturer's instructions to release pressure. Return pot to SAUTÉ (NORMAL). Stir in currants. Simmer stew, stirring often, until broth has reduced to a thick, flavorful gravy, about 10 minutes. Add vinegar. Stir in spinach by the handful. Season stew with additional salt and vinegar to taste.

15-Bean Soup

¼ cup nutritional yeast

4 dried bay leaves, crumbled

½ teaspoon celery seed

1 tablespoon smoked paprika

2 teaspoons chili powder

¼ cup olive oil

1 large onion, chopped

1 large green bell pepper, chopped

4 garlic cloves, chopped

Kosher salt and freshly ground black pepper

1½ pounds (20 ounces) mixed dried beans (or 20-ounce bag 15-Bean Soup®, seasoning packet discarded)

1 (14.5-ounce) can diced tomatoes

1 tablespoon cider vinegar, plus more to taste

In a spice grinder, combine yeast, bay leaves, and celery seed; process until finely ground. In a small bowl, stir together ground spices with paprika and chili powder; set aside. Set Instant Pot to SAUTÉ, and follow manufacturer's instructions to select middle temperature setting (NORMAL). Heat oil in metal insert until prompt indicates HOT; add onion, bell pepper, and garlic. Season with salt and pepper (about 1 teaspoon salt and ½ teaspoon pepper). Cook until vegetables have softened, about 5 minutes. Press CANCEL. Stir in reserved spices, beans, tomatoes, and 6 cups (1½ quarts) water. Season generously with salt (about 2 teaspoons). Close and lock the lid; seal valve (set to SEALING). Set to PRESSURE COOK with setting on HIGH. Set time to 15 minutes. When timer rings, press CANCEL; follow manufacturer's instructions to release pressure. Stir in vinegar. Season soup with additional vinegar and salt to taste.

Kinda Tortilla Soup

¼ cup hulled millet or coarse cornmeal (sometimes called "polenta")

1 large onion, quartered

6 cloves garlic, peeled

4 Anaheim or poblano peppers (about 1 pound)

Kosher salt

¼ cup avocado oil

1 large green bell pepper, chopped

2 tablespoons tomato paste

¼ cup Toasted Chili Powder (page 163) or store-bought

1 cup dried black beans (see note on page xi)

2 tablespoons firmly packed chopped cilantro leaves

1 tablespoon freshly squeezed lime juice, plus more to taste

Sliced ripe avocado for serving

Heat small, heavy skillet (such as cast-iron) over medium-high heat until hot (without oil); add millet. Roast, tossing, until millet is dark golden brown and fragrant, about 10 minutes. Grind millet in a spice grinder. Heat broiler with rack about 5 inches away from heat. Arrange onion, garlic, and whole Anaheim peppers on baking sheet; broil vegetables, turning once, until onions are charred and peppers are blistered in spots, about 10 minutes. Remove skins, stems, and seeds from peppers. Transfer vegetables to a blender jar with 1 cup water; blend, cracking lid and covering with a towel to release steam, until smooth. Season salsa mixture very generously with salt (about 2 teaspoons); set aside. Set Instant Pot to SAUTÉ, and follow manufacturer's instructions to select middle temperature setting (NORMAL). Heat oil in metal insert until prompt indicates HOT. Add bell pepper; season generously with salt (about 1 teaspoon). Cook, stirring often, until pepper has softened, about 10 minutes. Press CANCEL. Stir in reserved ground millet, tomato paste, chili powder, beans, reserved salsa mixture, and 5 cups (1¼ quarts) water; season generously with salt, about 1 teaspoon. Close and lock the lid; seal valve (set to SEALING). Set to PRESSURE COOK with setting on HIGH. Set time to 35 minutes. When timer rings, press CANCEL; follow manufacturer's instructions to release pressure. Stir in cilantro and lime juice. Season soup with additional salt and lime juice to taste. Serve soup with sliced avocado.

Thanksgiving Soup

1 large parsnip, peeled and cut into 1-inch disks

1 large carrot, peeled and cut into 1-inch disks

1 small celery root, peeled and cut into 1-inch pieces

1 small acorn squash, seeds removed and cut into 2-inch pieces (do not peel)

2 tablespoons olive oil, divided

¼ teaspoon ground nutmeg

Kosher salt and freshly ground black pepper

10 sage leaves, finely chopped

1 leek, white part only, halved lengthwise and sliced into ½-inch pieces

2 celery stalks, chopped

¼ cup nutritional yeast

1 cup wild rice, rinsed if desired

1 tablespoon cider vinegar, plus more to taste

Roasted hazelnuts, chopped, for serving, optional

Heat broiler with rack about 5 inches away from heat. On a large rimmed baking sheet, toss parsnip, carrot, celery root, and squash with 1 tablespoon oil and nutmeg. Season vegetables with salt and pepper (about ½ teaspoon salt and ¼ teaspoon pepper). Broil vegetables until brown in spots yet firm when pierced, about 8 minutes. While vegetables broil, combine sage and 1 tablespoon salt in a mortar; use a pestle to smash and grind salt and sage together until it forms greenish grit. Set Instant Pot to SAUTÉ, and follow manufacturer's instructions to select middle temperature setting (NORMAL). Heat remaining tablespoon oil in metal insert until prompt indicates HOT. Add leek and celery. Cook, stirring often, until vegetables are softened, about 10 minutes. Press CANCEL. Stir in yeast, rice, reserved vegetables and sage salt, and 6 cups (1½ quarts) water. Close and lock the lid; seal valve (set to SEALING). Set to PRESSURE COOK with setting on HIGH. Set time to 20 minutes. When timer rings, press CANCEL; follow manufacturer's instructions to release pressure. Stir in vinegar. Season soup with additional salt and vinegar to taste. Serve soup topped with hazelnuts, if desired.

Fennel Farinata

½ cup hulled millet or coarse cornmeal (sometimes called "polenta")

¼ cup olive oil

1 medium onion, chopped

2 celery stalks, chopped

1 medium carrot, peeled and chopped

1 small fennel bulb (with fronds preferred), cored and chopped (fronds, optional, reserved)

2 cloves garlic, chopped

Kosher salt and freshly ground black pepper

2 bay leaves, fresh or dried

1 cup dried chickpeas (see note on page xi)

1 small bunch kale, ribs and stems removed, thinly sliced

2 tablespoons chopped parsley

1 tablespoon freshly squeezed lemon juice, plus more to taste

Grind millet in a spice grinder or blender until powdery yet still coarse to the touch. Set Instant Pot to SAUTÉ, and follow manufacturer's instructions to select middle temperature setting (NORMAL). Heat oil in metal insert until prompt indicates HOT. Add onion, celery, carrot, fennel, and garlic; season generously with salt and pepper (about 1 teaspoon salt and ½ teaspoon pepper). Cook, stirring often, until vegetables are softened, about 10 minutes. While vegetables cook, if using fennel fronds, finely chop enough to make 2 tablespoons; set aside. Press CANCEL. Stir in bay leaves, chickpeas, kale, reserved millet, and 8 cups (2 quarts) water; season very generously with salt (about 2 teaspoons). Close and lock the lid; seal valve (set to SEALING). Set to PRESSURE COOK with setting on HIGH. Set time to 28 minutes. When timer rings, press CANCEL; follow manufacturer's instructions to release pressure. Stir in reserved fennel fronds (if using), parsley, and lemon juice. Season soup with additional salt and lemon juice to taste. Remove bay leaves before serving.

Ethiopian Lentil Soup

½ cup Vegan Nit'r Qibe (page 164)

1 medium onion, chopped

2 cloves garlic, finely chopped

Kosher salt

1 (14.5-ounce) can diced tomatoes

2 cups dried red lentils

2 teaspoons Homemade Berbere (page 164) or store-bought

1 tablespoon freshly squeezed lemon juice, plus more to taste

Cilantro leaves for serving, optional

Set Instant Pot to SAUTÉ, and follow manufacturer's instructions to select middle temperature setting (NORMAL). Heat nit'r qibe in metal insert until prompt indicates HOT. Add onion and garlic; season generously with salt (about 1 teaspoon). Cook, stirring often, until onion is beginning to soften but not browned, about 5 minutes. Press CANCEL. Stir in tomatoes, lentils, berbere, and 6 cups (1½ quarts) water; season with salt (about 1 teaspoon). Close and lock the lid; seal valve (set to SEALING). Set to PRESSURE COOK with setting on HIGH. Set time to 10 minutes. When timer rings, press CANCEL; follow manufacturer's instructions to release pressure. Stir in lemon juice. Season soup with additional salt and lemon juice to taste. Serve soup topped with cilantro, if desired.

West African Vegetable Stew

¼ cup avocado oil

1 medium onion, chopped

4 cloves garlic, chopped

1 (1-inch) piece fresh ginger, peeled and chopped

Kosher salt

2 tablespoons Homemade Curry Powder (page 162) or store-bought

⅛ teaspoon cayenne pepper

1 (28-ounce) can diced tomatoes

1 small bunch collard greens, ribs and stems removed, sliced into 1-inch strips (about 5 cups)

4 small (4 to 6-ounce) sweet potatoes or yams, peeled

8 ounces trimmed green beans, cut into 1-inch pieces (about 2 cups)

½ cup unsweetened sunflower seed, cashew, or peanut butter

1 cup roasted sunflower seeds, cashews, or peanuts, divided

1 tablespoon freshly squeezed lemon juice, plus more to taste

Set Instant Pot to SAUTÉ, and follow manufacturer's instructions to select middle temperature setting (NORMAL). Heat oil in metal insert until prompt indicates HOT. Add onion, garlic, and ginger; season generously with salt (about 1 teaspoon). Cook, stirring often, until onion has softened, about 10 minutes. Press CANCEL. Stir in curry powder, cayenne, tomatoes, collards, and 6 cups (1½ quarts) water; season very generously with salt (about 2 teaspoons). Add whole potatoes and beans to pot. Close and lock the lid; seal valve (set to SEALING). Set to PRESSURE COOK with setting on HIGH. Set time to 8 minutes. When timer rings, press CANCEL; follow manufacturer's instructions to release pressure. In a blender jar, place 1 cooked potato and 1 cup broth. Add sunflower seed butter; blend until smooth. Stir seed butter mixture back into stew to thicken. Stir in ½ cup sunflower seeds and lemon juice. Season stew with additional salt and lemon juice to taste. Break potatoes into large chunks before serving. Serve stew topped with a handful of sunflower seeds (or stir full amount into pot before serving).

Greek Soup Mashup

¼ cup olive oil

1 large onion, chopped

3 celery stalks, chopped

3 medium carrots, peeled and chopped

4 cloves garlic, finely chopped

Kosher salt and freshly ground black pepper

1 teaspoon dried oregano

2 tablespoons nutritional yeast

¾ cup short-grain brown rice

1 cup dried navy beans (see note on page xi)

¼ cup well-stirred tahini

¼ cup firmly packed chopped dill fronds

1 lemon

Set Instant Pot to SAUTÉ, and follow manufacturer's instructions to select middle temperature setting (NORMAL). Heat oil in metal insert until prompt indicates HOT. Add onion, celery, carrots, and garlic; season generously with salt and pepper (about 1 teaspoon salt and ½ teaspoon pepper). Cook, stirring often, until vegetables have softened, about 10 minutes. Press CANCEL. Stir in oregano, yeast, rice, beans, and 6 cups (1½ quarts) water; season very generously with salt (about 2 teaspoons). Close and lock the lid; seal valve (set to SEALING). Set to PRESSURE COOK with setting on HIGH. Set time to 22 minutes. When timer rings, press CANCEL; follow manufacturer's instructions to release pressure. Place tahini in a medium bowl; whisk in enough broth to loosen to a pourable consistency. Stir tahini mixture into soup with dill. Finely grate zest from lemon into soup (about 1 teaspoon); squeeze juice (about 2 tablespoons) into broth. Season soup with additional salt and pepper to taste.

Hoppin' John

1 (7-ounce) can chipotle chiles in adobo

8 sprigs thyme

1 tablespoon smoked paprika

2 bay leaves, fresh or dried

½ cup olive oil

1 large onion, chopped

1 large green bell pepper, chopped

1 medium carrot, peeled and chopped

Kosher salt

1 small bunch collard greens, ribs and stems removed, cut into 1-inch ribbons (about 5 cups)

1 pound dried black-eyed peas (see note on page xi)

1 (14.5-ounce) can fire-roasted diced tomatoes

2 tablespoons cider vinegar, plus more to taste

Cooked rice for serving

Remove 1 chipotle chile from can; remove stems (and seeds, for less heat) and chop. Place in a small bowl with 2 tablespoons adobo sauce. (Transfer remaining chiles and sauce to storage container; reserve for another use.) Add thyme, paprika, and bay leaves to small bowl with chile; set aside. Set Instant Pot to SAUTÉ, and follow manufacturer's instructions to select middle temperature setting (NORMAL). Heat oil in metal insert until prompt indicates HOT. Add onion, bell pepper, and carrot; season generously with salt (about 1 teaspoon). Cook, stirring often, until vegetables have softened, about 10 minutes. Press CANCEL. Stir in reserved spices, collards, beans, tomatoes, and 5 cups (1¼ quarts) water; season very generously with salt (about 2 teaspoons). Close and lock the lid; seal valve (set to SEALING). Set to PRESSURE COOK with setting on HIGH. Set time to 32 minutes. When timer rings, press CANCEL; follow manufacturer's instructions to release pressure. Stir in vinegar. Season soup with additional salt and vinegar to taste. Remove bay leaves and thyme stems before serving. Serve soup over rice.

Minestrone Invernale

2 heads garlic

4 sprigs rosemary, divided

¼ cup olive oil, divided

Kosher salt and freshly ground black pepper

1 medium onion, chopped

2 inner celery stalks with their leaves, chopped

2 medium carrots, peeled and chopped

1 small bunch Swiss Chard, leaves shredded (4 cups) and stems roughly chopped (about 1 cup)

2 tablespoons Dijon mustard

1 cup dried cranberry or pinto beans (see note on page xi)

1 (14.5-ounce) can diced tomatoes

1 small head radicchio, halved, cored, and shredded (about 4 cups)

1 small bunch Lacinato kale, ribs and stems removed, roughly torn (about 2 cups)

1 cup rotini pasta (gluten-free or traditional), chopped or broken into small pieces, optional

Preheat oven to 350°F. Slice into heads of garlic crosswise, removing the topmost ¾ inch to just expose the raw cloves. Place garlic on a double thickness of aluminum foil (lined with parchment, if desired) with 1 sprig rosemary. Drizzle with 1 tablespoon oil; season with salt and pepper (about ½ teaspoon salt and ¼ teaspoon pepper). Gather edges of foil to enclose garlic and rosemary; place packet on a rimmed baking sheet. Bake until packet is fragrant and sizzling and cloves are golden and risen from their papers, about 1½ hours. Set aside until cool enough to handle, about 20 minutes. Squeeze garlic from their papers into a small bowl. (You should have about ⅓ cup garlic paste.) Set Instant Pot to SAUTÉ, and follow manufacturer's instructions to select middle temperature setting (NORMAL). Heat remaining oil in metal insert until prompt indicates HOT. Add onion, celery, carrots, and chard stems; season generously with salt and pepper (about 1 teaspoon salt and ½ teaspoon pepper). Cook, stirring often, until vegetables have softened, about 10 minutes. Press CANCEL. Stir in reserved garlic, remaining rosemary sprigs, mustard, beans, tomatoes, and half each chard leaves (2 cups), radicchio (2 cups), and kale (1 cup), and 6 cups (1½ quarts) water; season very generously with salt (about 2 teaspoons). Close and lock the lid; seal valve (set to SEALING). Set to PRESSURE COOK with setting on HIGH. Set time to 30 minutes. When timer rings, press CANCEL; follow manufacturer's instructions to release pressure. Stir in remaining greens and pasta. Return lid to pot and let stand until greens and pasta are softened, about 20 minutes. Season soup with additional salt to taste. Remove rosemary sprigs before serving.

Jamaican Pumpkin + Red Pea Soup

4 cloves garlic

1 jalapeño, seeds and membrane removed for less heat, roughly chopped

1 (1-inch) piece fresh ginger

1 bunch scallions (both whites and greens), chopped

1 medium onion, quartered

1 teaspoon ground allspice

1 teaspoon ground cinnamon

1 small bunch thyme, stripped (about 2 teaspoons leaves)

Kosher salt and freshly ground black pepper

¼ cup coconut oil

1 cup dried small red beans (see note on page xi)

2 medium carrots, peeled and cut into 1-inch pieces

1 small bunch collard greens, ribs and stems removed, sliced into 1-inch strips (about 5 cups)

½ medium calabaza, hubbard, or kabocha squash (about 3½ pounds), peeled, seeds removed, and cut into very large (3-inch) chunks

1 cup full-fat coconut cream (from a well-shaken carton, such as Aroy-D brand; sold at Asian markets)

1 tablespoon coconut sugar

2 tablespoons freshly squeezed lime juice, plus more to taste

Lime wedges for serving

In a blender, combine garlic, jalapeño, ginger, scallions, onion, allspice, cinnamon, thyme, ½ teaspoon pepper, and ¼ cup water; blend until smooth. Set Instant Pot to SAUTÉ, and follow manufacturer's instructions to select middle temperature setting (NORMAL). Heat oil in metal insert until prompt indicates HOT. Carefully add reserved onion paste (it will spatter); season generously with salt (about 1 teaspoon). Cook, stirring often, until mixture has thickened and darkened, about 8 minutes. Press CANCEL. Stir in beans, carrots, collards, squash, and 6 cups (1½ quarts) water; season very generously with salt (about 2 teaspoons). Close and lock the lid; seal valve (set to SEALING). Set to PRESSURE COOK with setting on HIGH. Set time to 30 minutes. When timer rings, press CANCEL; follow manufacturer's instructions to release pressure. Stir in coconut cream, coconut sugar, and lime juice. Season soup with additional salt and lime juice to taste. Serve soup with lime wedges.

Golden Borscht

¼ cup olive oil

1 small onion, chopped

2 celery stalks, chopped

1 garlic clove, chopped

1 teaspoon caraway seeds

¼ teaspoon ground turmeric, optional

Kosher salt and freshly ground black pepper

1 pound carrots (about 6 medium), peeled and cut into 1-inch pieces

1 pound yellow beets (about 2 medium), peeled and cut into 1-inch chunks

1 pound white sweet potato (about 1 large), cut into 2-inch chunks

½ small Savoy or green cabbage, cored and cut into 1-inch pieces (about 4 cups)

1 bay leaf, fresh or dried

¼ cup cider vinegar, plus more to taste

¼ cup firmly packed chopped dill fronds

¼ cup firmly packed chopped parsley

Sour cream or Greek yogurt for serving, optional

Set Instant Pot to SAUTÉ, and follow manufacturer's instructions to select middle temperature setting (NORMAL). Heat oil in metal insert until prompt indicates HOT. Add onion, celery, garlic, caraway, and turmeric (if using); season generously with salt and pepper (about 1 teaspoon salt and ½ teaspoon pepper). Cook, stirring often, until onion has softened, about 10 minutes. Press CANCEL. Stir in carrots, beets, potato, cabbage, bay leaf, vinegar, and 6 cups (1½ quarts) water; season very generously with salt (about 2 teaspoons). Close and lock the lid; seal valve (set to SEALING). Set to PRESSURE COOK with setting on HIGH. Set time to 15 minutes. When timer rings, press CANCEL; follow manufacturer's instructions to release pressure. Stir in dill and parsley. Season stew with additional salt and vinegar to taste. Remove bay leaf before serving. Serve topped with a generous dollop of sour cream or Greek yogurt, if desired.

Asparagus, Dill + Lemon Soup

¼ cup olive oil

1 medium leek (white and light green part only), halved lengthwise and sliced

2 celery stalks, chopped

1 medium carrot, peeled and chopped

1 bunch scallions, white and greens chopped separately

Kosher salt

1 medium turnip, peeled and cut into 1-inch pieces

½ small Savoy or green cabbage, cored, quartered, and sliced into ½-inch ribbons

½ cup sorghum, rinsed if desired

1 bunch asparagus (about 1 pound), trimmed of woody ends and cut into 1-inch pieces

1 lemon

¼ cup firmly packed chopped dill fronds

¼ cup firmly packed chopped chervil, optional

Set Instant Pot to SAUTÉ, and follow manufacturer's instructions to select middle temperature setting (NORMAL). Heat oil in metal insert until prompt indicates HOT. Add leek, celery, carrot, and scallions (whites only; set aside greens to use later); season generously with salt (about 1 teaspoon). Cook, stirring often, until vegetables have softened, about 10 minutes. Press CANCEL. Stir in turnip, cabbage, sorghum, and 6 cups (1½ quarts) water; season very generously with salt (about 2 teaspoons). Close and lock the lid; seal valve (set to SEALING). Set to PRESSURE COOK with setting on HIGH. Set time to 22 minutes. When timer rings, press CANCEL; follow manufacturer's instructions to release pressure. Return pot to SAUTÉ (NORMAL). Stir in asparagus. Simmer soup until asparagus is crisp, bright green, and tender, about 2 minutes. Finely grate zest of lemon over soup (about 1 teaspoon); squeeze juice into soup (about 2 tablespoons). Stir in reserved scallion greens, dill, and chervil (if using). Season soup with additional salt and lemon juice to taste.

Harira

½ cup olive oil

1 medium onion, chopped

1 (1-inch) piece fresh ginger, peeled and chopped

Kosher salt

1 teaspoon dried turmeric

1 (3-inch) piece cinnamon stick

1 (14.5-ounce) can diced tomatoes

1 cup dried chickpeas (see note on page xi)

1 cup green (French) lentils

½ cup long-grain brown rice

2 tablespoons tomato paste

2 tablespoons chickpea flour (sometimes called "besan") or all-purpose flour

¼ cup chopped cilantro leaves

2 tablespoons freshly squeezed lemon juice, plus more to taste

Set Instant Pot to SAUTÉ, and follow manufacturer's instructions to select middle temperature setting (NORMAL). Heat oil in metal insert until prompt indicates HOT. Add onion and ginger; season generously with salt (about 1 teaspoon). Cook, stirring often, until onion has softened, about 10 minutes. Press CANCEL. Stir in turmeric, cinnamon, tomatoes, chickpeas, lentils, rice, and 6 cups (1½ quarts) water; season very generously with salt (about 2 teaspoons). Close and lock the lid; seal valve (set to SEALING). Set to PRESSURE COOK with setting on HIGH. Set time to 30 minutes. While soup cooks, whisk together tomato paste, flour, cilantro, lemon juice, and ¼ cup water in a small bowl; season generously with salt (about 1 teaspoon). When timer rings, press CANCEL; follow manufacturer's instructions to release pressure. Return pot to SAUTÉ (NORMAL). Once broth has returned to a simmer, whisk in flour mixture. Simmer soup, stirring constantly, until broth thickens (about 3 minutes). Season soup with additional salt and lemon juice to taste.

Gumbo Z'Herbes

¼ cup olive oil

¼ cup chickpea flour (sometimes called "besan")

1 large onion, chopped

1 large green bell pepper, chopped

2 celery stalks, chopped

6 cloves garlic, finely chopped

Kosher salt

2 tablespoons Homemade Cajun Seasoning (page 165) or store-bought

2 bay leaves, fresh or dried

1 pound fresh or frozen okra, cut into 1-inch pieces

1 small bunch mustard greens, ribs and stems removed, roughly torn (about 4 cups)

1 bunch parsley (including stems), chopped

1 tablespoon cider vinegar, plus more to taste

5 cups baby spinach (5-ounce container)

Cooked rice for serving, optional

Set Instant Pot to SAUTÉ, and follow manufacturer's instructions to select middle temperature setting (NORMAL). Heat oil in metal insert until prompt indicates HOT. Add flour and cook, stirring often, until it turns a deep coppery brown, about 12 minutes. Stir in onion, bell pepper, celery, and garlic; season generously with salt (about 1 teaspoon). Cook, stirring occasionally, until vegetables have softened, about 10 minutes. Press CANCEL. Stir in Cajun seasoning, bay leaves, okra, mustard greens, parsley, and 4 cups (1 quart) water, taking care to scrape and release any browned bits that stuck to the bottom of the insert; season very generously with salt (about 2 teaspoons). Close and lock the lid; seal valve (set to SEALING). Set to PRESSURE COOK with setting on HIGH. Set time to 10 minutes. When timer rings, press CANCEL; follow manufacturer's instructions to release pressure. Return pot to SAUTÉ (NORMAL). Simmer soup, stirring constantly and mashing okra to thicken broth, until it is thick, about 5 minutes. Add vinegar. Stir in spinach by the handful. Season soup with salt and additional vinegar to taste. Remove bay leaves before serving. Serve soup over rice, if desired.

Nearly Retro Cabbage Soup

½ cup coconut oil, divided

1 medium head green cabbage, quartered (core intact)

Kosher salt and freshly ground black pepper

1 medium onion, chopped

2 celery stalks, sliced ½ inch thick

4 cloves garlic, finely chopped

1 (1-inch) piece fresh ginger, peeled and chopped

2 tablespoons tomato paste

2 medium carrots, peeled and cut into 1-inch pieces

8 ounces Brussels sprouts, quartered

1 cup dried butter beans (see note on page xi)

1 (14.5-ounce) can fire-roasted diced tomatoes

1 tablespoon coconut aminos, plus more to taste

1 tablespoon freshly squeezed lemon juice, plus more to taste

Heat half of oil in a large, heavy skillet (such as cast-iron) over medium-high heat until very hot (it will smoke). Sear cabbage until it's a deep caramel color on both sides, about 8 minutes total. Transfer cabbage to a cutting board to cool 5 minutes; season with salt and pepper (about ½ teaspoon each salt and pepper). Set Instant Pot to SAUTÉ, and follow manufacturer's instructions to select middle temperature setting (NORMAL). Pour leftover oil from skillet into insert with remaining oil and heat until prompt indicates HOT. Add onion, celery, garlic, and ginger; season generously with salt (about 1 teaspoon). Cook, stirring often, until vegetables are softened, about 10 minutes. Slice away core of cabbage and cut into 2-inch pieces. Stir in tomato paste, carrots, Brussels sprouts, beans, tomatoes, reserved cabbage, and 6 cups (1½ quarts) water; season very generously with salt (about 2 teaspoons). Press CANCEL. Close and lock the lid; seal valve (set to SEALING). Set to PRESSURE COOK with setting on HIGH. Set time to 27 minutes. When timer rings, press CANCEL; follow manufacturer's instructions to release pressure. Stir in coconut aminos and lemon juice. Season soup with additional salt, coconut aminos, and lemon juice to taste.

Persian Herb and Noodle Soup

½ cup olive oil

1 medium onion, chopped

4 cloves garlic, finely chopped

Kosher salt and freshly ground black pepper

¼ cup nutritional yeast

1 teaspoon dried turmeric

1 cup dried navy beans (see note on page xi)

½ cup dried brown lentils

5 cups baby spinach (5-ounce container), roughly chopped

2 bunches parsley (including stems), roughly chopped

2 bunches cilantro (including stems), roughly chopped

1 large bunch dill (fronds only), roughly chopped

2 large (about 1-inch-thick) bunches chives, roughly chopped

1 cup mint leaves (stripped from about 15 sprigs)

8 ounces spaghetti (gluten-free or traditional), broken in half

2 tablespoons lemon juice, plus more to taste

Greek yogurt for serving, optional

Set Instant Pot to SAUTÉ, and follow manufacturer's instructions to select middle temperature setting (NORMAL). Heat oil in metal insert until prompt indicates HOT. Add onion and garlic; season generously with salt and pepper (about 1 teaspoon salt and ½ teaspoon pepper). Cook, stirring often, until onion has softened, about 10 minutes. Press CANCEL. Stir in yeast, turmeric, beans, lentils, spinach, parsley, cilantro, dill, chives, mint, and 6 cups (1½ quarts) water; season very generously with salt (about 2 teaspoons). (Insert will be very full.) Close and lock the lid; seal valve (set to SEALING). Set to PRESSURE COOK with setting on HIGH. Set time to 15 minutes. When timer rings, press CANCEL; follow manufacturer's instructions to release pressure. Scatter pasta over top of soup in one or two layers; pour 1 cup water over pasta (do not stir). Return lid to pot. Close and lock the lid; seal valve (set to SEALING). Return pot to PRESSURE COOK with setting on HIGH. Set time to 8 minutes. When timer rings, press CANCEL; use quick release to release pressure. Stir in lemon juice and use spoon to separate cooked noodles. Season soup with additional salt and lemon juice to taste. Serve soup topped with Greek yogurt, if desired.

Cream of Mushroom Soup

1 ounce dried porcini mushrooms, chopped or broken into small pieces (about ¾ cup)

⅓ cup nutritional yeast

Kosher salt and freshly ground black pepper

½ cup gluten-free rolled oats

¼ cup olive oil

1 medium onion, chopped

2 cloves garlic, finely chopped

1 pound cremini mushrooms, trimmed of dry stems and quartered (about 4 cups)

8 ounces oyster mushrooms, trimmed of dry stems and roughly chopped (about 3 cups)

8 ounces shiitake mushrooms, trimmed of dry stems and roughly chopped (about 3 cups)

2 sprigs rosemary

2 bay leaves, fresh or dried

½ cup well-stirred tahini

2 teaspoons vegan Worcestershire sauce

1 tablespoon sherry or cider vinegar, plus more to taste

In a blender jar, combine dried mushrooms, yeast, and 1 tablespoon salt; process until finely ground, about 1 minute. Transfer mushroom salt to a bowl and set aside; reserve blender jar. Heat a medium, heavy skillet (such as cast-iron) over medium heat until hot (without oil); add oats. Roast oats, stirring often, until golden brown and fragrant, about 3 minutes; transfer to a bowl and set aside. Set Instant Pot to SAUTÉ, and follow manufacturer's instructions to select middle temperature setting (NORMAL). Heat oil in metal insert until prompt indicates HOT. Add onion and garlic; season generously with salt and pepper (about 1 teaspoon salt and ½ teaspoon pepper). Cook, stirring often, until onion has softened, about 10 minutes. Stir in fresh mushrooms; cook, stirring often, until they begin to release their liquid, about 5 minutes. Press CANCEL. Stir in reserved mushroom salt, rosemary, bay leaves, and 6 cups (1½ quarts) water. Close and lock the lid; seal valve (set to SEALING). Set to PRESSURE COOK with setting on HIGH. Set time to 5 minutes. When timer rings, press CANCEL; follow manufacturer's instructions to release pressure. Remove 2 cups mushroom broth from soup; transfer to reserved blender jar with reserved toasted oats, tahini, and Worcestershire; blend until smooth, about 1 minute. Return setting to SAUTÉ. Simmer soup, stirring often, until broth is smooth and thick and mushrooms are fully cooked, about 5 minutes. Stir in vinegar. Season soup with additional salt and vinegar to taste. Remove rosemary sprigs and bay leaves before serving.

Broccoli and Rice Soup

1 large bunch broccoli with long stalks (about 1 pound)

½ cup dried mung beans

¼ cup olive oil

1 medium onion, chopped

2 teaspoons ground coriander

Kosher salt and freshly ground black pepper

1 bunch scallions (both whites and greens), chopped

¼ cup nutritional yeast

1 bunch baby broccoli, sliced into 1-inch pieces (about 5 cups)

½ cup short-grain brown rice

¼ cup cilantro leaves, chopped

1 tablespoon lemon juice, plus more to taste

Cut broccoli to separate stalks from crowns; peel outer, rough layer from stalks with a vegetable peeler and roughly chop. Break and cut broccoli crowns into florets ranging from 1 to 3 inches at the widest part. (You should have about 4 cups broccoli florets and 1 to 2 cups chopped broccoli.) Heat a medium, heavy skillet (such as cast-iron) over medium heat until hot (without oil); add beans. Roast beans, stirring often, until golden brown, about 5 minutes. Transfer beans to a parchment-lined baking sheet in a single layer; set aside until cool to the touch, about 3 minutes. Use parchment to funnel beans into a spice grinder or blender; process until finely ground. (You should have about ½ cup ground beans.) Set Instant Pot to SAUTÉ, and follow manufacturer's instructions to select middle temperature setting (NORMAL). Heat oil in metal insert until prompt indicates HOT. Add onion and coriander; season generously with salt and pepper (about 1 teaspoon salt and ½ teaspoon pepper). Cook, stirring often, until onion has softened, about 10 minutes. Press CANCEL. Stir in ground beans, reserved florets and chopped broccoli stalks, scallions, yeast, baby broccoli, rice, and 8 cups (2 quarts) water; season very generously with salt (about 2 teaspoons). Close and lock the lid; seal valve (set to SEALING). Set to PRESSURE COOK with setting on HIGH. Set time to 8 minutes. When timer rings, press CANCEL; follow manufacturer's instructions to release pressure. Stir in cilantro and lemon juice. Season soup with additional salt and lemon juice to taste.

Peas 'n' Carrots Soup

8 ounces sugar snap peas, strings discarded, halved

4 large carrots, peeled and cut into 1-inch pieces

4 cloves garlic, sliced

¼ cup olive oil, divided

2 teaspoons ground sumac

Kosher salt and freshly ground black pepper

1 medium onion, chopped

2 celery stalks, chopped

1 (1-inch) piece fresh ginger, peeled and chopped

1 cup dried chickpeas (see note on page xi)

1 (14.5-ounce) can fire-roasted diced tomatoes

2 cups frozen green peas

1 tablespoon cider vinegar, plus more to taste

5 cups baby spinach (5-ounce container)

Heat broiler with rack about 5 inches away from heat. On a large rimmed baking sheet, toss snap peas, carrots, and garlic with 1 tablespoon oil and sumac; season generously with salt and pepper (about 1 teaspoon salt and ½ teaspoon pepper). Broil vegetables, tossing once, until browned in spots yet firm when pierced, about 4 minutes. Set Instant Pot to SAUTÉ, and follow manufacturer's instructions to select middle temperature setting (NORMAL). Heat remaining oil in metal insert until prompt indicates HOT. Add onion and celery; season generously with salt and pepper (about 1 teaspoon salt and ½ teaspoon pepper). Cook, stirring often, until onion is beginning to soften but not browned, about 5 minutes. Press CANCEL. Stir in reserved broiled vegetables, ginger, chickpeas, tomatoes, and 6 cups (1½ quarts) water; season generously with salt (about 1 teaspoon). Close and lock the lid; seal valve (set to SEALING). Set to PRESSURE COOK with setting on HIGH. Set time to 30 minutes. When timer rings, press CANCEL; follow manufacturer's instructions to release pressure. Stir in peas and vinegar. Stir in spinach by the handful. Season soup with additional salt and vinegar to taste.

Teddy's Black Bean Soup

1 cup olive oil

1 large onion, chopped

1 large green bell pepper, chopped

Kosher salt

6 cloves garlic, finely chopped

1 tablespoon ground cumin

1 tablespoon dried oregano

2 tablespoons cider vinegar, plus more to taste

1 pound dried black beans (see note on page xi)

Set Instant Pot to SAUTÉ, and follow manufacturer's instructions to select middle temperature setting (NORMAL). Heat oil in metal insert until prompt indicates HOT. Add onion and bell pepper; season generously with salt (about 1 teaspoon). Cook, stirring often, until vegetables have softened, about 10 minutes. Stir in garlic, cumin, oregano, vinegar, beans, and 5 cups (1¼ quarts) water; season very generously with salt (about 2 teaspoons). Press CANCEL. Close and lock the lid; seal valve (set to SEALING). Set to PRESSURE COOK with setting on HIGH. Set time to 35 minutes. When timer rings, press CANCEL; follow manufacturer's instructions to release pressure. Return pot to SAUTÉ (NORMAL). Simmer soup, stirring constantly and mashing beans to create a cloudy gravy, until it is thick, about 10 minutes. Season soup with additional salt and vinegar to taste.

Portuguese Pea Stew

1 large red bell pepper

¼ cup olive oil

1 medium onion, chopped

4 cloves garlic, chopped

Kosher salt and freshly ground black pepper

1 tablespoon smoked paprika

1 (4-inch) piece cinnamon stick

1 bay leaf, fresh or dried

1 small bunch cilantro (stems included), chopped

1 cup dried split peas

1 (14.5-ounce) can diced tomatoes

1 (12-ounce) bag frozen peas

1 tablespoon freshly squeezed lemon juice, plus more to taste

Heat broiler with rack in highest position. Place bell pepper directly on rack; broil pepper, turning often, until it is blistered and entirely charred, about 10 minutes total. Transfer pepper to a bowl; cover with a plate or pot lid. Set aside until cool enough to handle, about 8 minutes. Remove skin, stem, and seeds from pepper; roughly chop. (You should have about 1 cup chopped roasted pepper.) Set Instant Pot to SAUTÉ, and follow manufacturer's instructions to select middle temperature setting (NORMAL). Heat oil in metal insert until prompt indicates HOT. Add onion and garlic; season generously with salt and pepper (about 1 teaspoon salt and ½ teaspoon pepper). Cook, stirring often, until onion is beginning to soften but not browned, about 5 minutes. Press CANCEL. Stir in reserved roasted pepper, paprika, cinnamon, bay leaf, cilantro, split peas, tomatoes, and 6 cups (1½ quarts) water; season very generously with salt (about 2 teaspoons). Close and lock the lid; seal valve (set to SEALING). Set to PRESSURE COOK with setting on HIGH. Set time to 20 minutes. When timer rings, press CANCEL; follow manufacturer's instructions to release pressure. Return pot to SAUTÉ (NORMAL). Simmer stew, stirring occasionally, until broth is thick and cloudy, about 10 minutes. Stir in frozen peas and lemon juice. Season stew with additional salt and lemon juice to taste. Remove bay leaf and cinnamon stick before serving.

Seattle Springtime Lentil Soup

2 pints cherry tomatoes

4 medium carrots, peeled and sliced into ½-inch disks

1 bunch scallions (both whites and greens), sliced ½ inch thick

¼ cup coconut oil, melted until liquid, divided

Kosher salt

1 (1-inch) piece fresh ginger, roughly chopped

2 cloves garlic, peeled

1 tablespoon Homemade Curry Powder (page 162) or store-bought

2 tablespoons nigella seeds (sometimes called "kalongi," "black cumin," or "black caraway")

1 (28-ounce) can crushed tomatoes

1 cup dried black lentils

1 tablespoon freshly squeezed lime juice, plus more to taste

1 cup full-fat coconut cream (from a well-shaken carton, such as Aroy-D brand; sold at Asian markets)

5 cups baby or "wild" arugula (5-ounce container)

Preheat oven to 425°F with racks dividing oven into upper and lower thirds. Line 2 large rimmed baking sheets with parchment. Place tomatoes on one prepared baking sheet, and mix carrots and scallions on the other. Drizzle contents of each baking sheet with 1 tablespoon oil and season with salt (about ½ teaspoon per sheet); toss to coat vegetables in oil. Roast vegetables without tossing, swapping pans halfway through, until tomatoes have withered and released their juices and the carrots are tender when pierced with a knife, about 20 minutes. Transfer ½ cup roasted tomatoes to a bowl; set aside. Use parchment to slide remaining vegetables into a blender with ginger, garlic, and 2 cups water; blend until smooth. Pour vegetable purée into metal insert with remaining oil. Stir in curry powder, nigella seeds, tomatoes, lentils, and 3 cups (¾ quart) water; season very generously with salt (about 2 teaspoons). Close and lock the lid; seal valve (set to SEALING). Set to PRESSURE COOK with setting on HIGH. Set time to 20 minutes. When timer rings, press CANCEL; follow manufacturer's instructions to release pressure. Add lime juice and half coconut cream; stir in arugula by the handful. Season soup with additional lime juice and salt to taste. Serve soup drizzled with remaining coconut cream and topped with a few roasted tomatoes (or stir full amount of cream and tomatoes into pot before serving).

Spring Minestrone

3 Meyer lemons

Kosher salt

1 bunch radishes with greens (about 10), thoroughly washed

1 large bunch ramps, spring onions, or scallions (about 6 ounces)

¼ cup olive oil

1 medium onion, chopped

2 celery stalks, chopped

1 medium carrot, peeled and chopped

1 large bunch dandelion greens, leaves thickly sliced (4 cups) and stems roughly chopped (about 1 cup)

1 cup dried pink or pinto beans (see note on page xi)

4 sprigs thyme

1 cup risoni or orzo pasta (gluten-free or traditional)

1 tablespoon agave nectar, plus more to taste

Finely grate zest from lemons; halve and squeeze juice from fruit. (You should have about 1 tablespoon zest and 3 tablespoons juice.) Combine lemon zest and 1 tablespoon salt in a mortar; use a pestle to smash and grind salt and zest together until it forms yellowish grit. (Alternatively, add salt to pile of lemon zest on a cutting board; chop and use side of knife to smash salt and zest together.) Halve radishes and finely chop greens. Prepare ramps: Separate ramp greens from bulbs; chop separately. (You should have at least ½ cup firmly packed whites and 1 to 2 cups firmly packed greens.) Set Instant Pot to SAUTÉ, and follow manufacturer's instructions to select middle temperature setting (NORMAL). Heat oil in metal insert until prompt indicates HOT. Add onion, celery, carrot, ramps (whites only), and half reserved Meyer lemon salt. Cook, stirring often, until vegetables have softened, about 10 minutes. Press CANCEL. Stir in reserved radish bulbs, dandelion greens, beans, thyme, and 6 cups (1½ quarts) water; season generously with salt (about 1 teaspoon). Close and lock the lid; seal valve (set to SEALING). Set to PRESSURE COOK with setting on HIGH. Set time to 28 minutes. When timer rings, press CANCEL; follow manufacturer's instructions to release pressure. Stir in reserved radish and ramp greens, remaining Meyer lemon salt and pasta. Return lid to pot and let stand until greens and pasta are softened, about 20 minutes. Stir in 2 tablespoons reserved lemon juice and agave. Season soup with additional salt, lemon juice, and agave to taste. Remove thyme sprigs before serving.

Summer Succotash Soup

½ cup olive oil

1 large sweet onion, chopped

1 large green bell pepper, chopped

3 large red, yellow, or orange bell peppers, chopped

2 cloves garlic, chopped

Kosher salt

2 tablespoons yellow or brown mustard seeds

1 tablespoon smoked paprika

¼ teaspoon red pepper flakes

4 sprigs thyme

1 pound dried black-eyed peas (see note on page xi)

1½ pounds unripe green tomatoes or tomatillos, husk removed, roughly chopped

½ cup firmly packed basil leaves (from 1 bunch), roughly torn

Cornbread for serving

Set Instant Pot to SAUTÉ, and follow manufacturer's instructions to select middle temperature setting (NORMAL). Heat oil in metal insert until prompt indicates HOT. Add onion, bell peppers, and garlic; season generously with salt (about 1 teaspoon). Cook, stirring often, until vegetables have softened, about 10 minutes. Press CANCEL. Stir in mustard seeds, paprika, pepper flakes, thyme, black-eyed peas, tomatoes, and 6 cups (1½ quarts) water; season very generously with salt (about 2 teaspoons). Close and lock the lid; seal valve (set to Sealing). Set to PRESSURE COOK with setting on HIGH. Set time to 35 minutes. When timer rings, press CANCEL; follow manufacturer's instructions to release pressure. Stir in basil. Season soup with additional salt to taste. Remove thyme sprigs before serving. Serve with cornbread.

Chunky Garden Vegetable Stew

¼ cup olive oil

1 medium onion, chopped

2 celery stalks, cut into 1-inch pieces

2 cloves garlic, chopped

Kosher salt and freshly ground black pepper

1 bay leaf, fresh or dried

½ teaspoon dried turmeric

2 tablespoons nutritional yeast

1 (28-ounce) can crushed tomatoes

8 ounces green beans, cut into 1-inch pieces (about 2 cups)

1 medium white sweet potato, peeled and cut into 1-inch pieces (about 2 cups)

3 large carrots, peeled and cut into 1-inch chunks

1 cup dried mung beans

1 medium yellow squash, quartered lengthwise and sliced into 1-inch chunks

1 cup frozen peas

1 tablespoon cider vinegar, plus more to taste

Heat oil in metal insert until prompt indicates HOT. Add onion, celery, and garlic; season generously with salt and pepper (about 1 teaspoon salt and ½ teaspoon pepper). Cook, stirring often, until vegetables have softened, about 10 minutes. Press CANCEL. Stir in bay leaf, turmeric, yeast, tomatoes, beans, potato, carrots, mung beans, and 6 cups (1¼ quarts) water; season very generously with salt (about 2 teaspoons). Close and lock the lid; seal valve (set to SEALING). Set to PRESSURE COOK with setting on HIGH. Set time to 25 minutes. When timer rings, press CANCEL; follow manufacturer's instructions to release pressure. Add squash and peas. Return lid to pot and let stand until squash has softened, about 10 minutes. Stir in vinegar. Season soup with additional salt and vinegar to taste. Remove bay leaf before serving.

Alabama Summer Garden Soup

¼ cup olive oil

1 large sweet or yellow onion, chopped

2 carrots, peeled and chopped

2 celery stalks, chopped

1 red bell pepper, chopped

1 garlic clove, finely chopped

Kosher salt and freshly ground black pepper

1 cup dried pigeon peas (soaked overnight) or dried black-eyed peas (see note on page xi)

1 small bunch mustard greens, ribs and stems removed, roughly torn (about 4 cups)

1 pound ripe Roma tomatoes (about 6), halved lengthwise

2 medium yellow squash (about 1 pound), halved lengthwise and sliced into ½-inch crescents

4 ounces fresh okra (about 6), cut into 1-inch pieces

½ teaspoon Tabasco or pepper vinegar sauce, plus more to taste

1 teaspoon cider vinegar, plus more to taste

Set Instant Pot to SAUTÉ, and follow manufacturer's instructions to select middle temperature setting (NORMAL). Heat oil in metal insert until prompt indicates HOT. Add onion, carrots, celery, bell pepper, and garlic; season generously with salt and pepper (about 1 teaspoon salt and ½ teaspoon pepper). Cook, stirring often, until vegetables have softened, about 10 minutes. Press CANCEL. Stir in pigeon peas, mustard greens, and 8 cups (2 quarts) water; season very generously with salt (about 2 teaspoons). Close and lock the lid; seal valve (set to SEALING). Set to PRESSURE COOK with setting on HIGH. Set time to 30 minutes. While soup cooks, coarsely grate cut-side of tomatoes; set pulp aside and compost tomato skins. (You should have 1 heaping cup fresh tomato pulp.) When timer rings, press CANCEL; follow manufacturer's instructions to release pressure. Stir in squash, okra, and reserved tomato pulp. Return pot to SAUTÉ (NORMAL). Simmer soup, stirring often, until squash and okra are just cooked through, about 5 minutes. Stir in Tabasco and vinegar. Season soup with additional salt, Tabasco, and vinegar to taste.

Louisiana Red Bean Soup

1 (7-ounce) can chipotle chiles in adobo

½ cup avocado oil

1 large onion, chopped

1 large green bell pepper, chopped

2 celery stalks, chopped

4 cloves garlic, finely chopped

Kosher salt

2 tablespoons Homemade Cajun Seasoning (page 165) or store-bought

1 tablespoon smoked paprika

2 bay leaves, fresh or dried

1 pound dried small red beans (see note on page xi)

1 tablespoon cider vinegar, plus more to taste

Cooked rice for serving

Remove 1 chile from can; remove stems (and seeds, for less heat) and chop. Place in small bowl with 2 tablespoons adobo sauce. (Transfer remaining chiles and sauce to storage container; reserve for another use.) Set Instant Pot to SAUTÉ, and follow manufacturer's instructions to select middle temperature setting (NORMAL). Heat oil in metal insert until prompt indicates HOT. Stir in onion, bell pepper, celery, and garlic; season generously with salt (about 1 teaspoon). Cook, stirring often, until vegetables have softened, about 10 minutes. Press CANCEL. Add reserved chile, Cajun seasoning, paprika, bay leaves, beans, and 6 cups (1½ quarts) water; season very generously with salt (about 2 teaspoons). Close and lock the lid; seal valve (set to SEALING). Set to PRESSURE COOK with setting on HIGH. Set time to 38 minutes. When timer rings, press CANCEL; follow manufacturer's instructions to release pressure. Return pot to SAUTÉ (NORMAL). Simmer soup, stirring constantly and mashing beans to create a cloudy gravy, until it is thick, about 10 minutes. Stir in vinegar. Season soup with additional salt and vinegar to taste. Remove bay leaves before serving. Serve soup over rice.

Farmer's Market Pistou

½ bunch carrots with greens (about 4)

4 sheets dried lasagna noodles (gluten-free or traditional)

2 large heirloom tomatoes, cored and quartered

1 garlic clove, peeled

Kosher salt and freshly ground black pepper

¼ cup olive oil

1 sweet onion, chopped

2 celery stalks, chopped

4 ounces wax beans, sliced into 1-inch pieces

4 ounces green beans, sliced into 1-inch pieces

1 cup dried Great Northern beans (see note on page xi)

1 bay leaf, fresh or dried

4 sprigs thyme

1 pound summer squash, such as yellow, pattypan, or zucchini, cut into 1-inch pieces

½ cup Vegan Pesto (page 164) or store-bought for serving

Peel and chop carrots. Wash, dry, and finely chop carrot greens (leafy fronds only; compost long stalks). (You should have about ½ cup chopped carrot greens.) Snap noodles into approximately 2-inch pieces. In a blender jar, combine tomatoes, garlic, and 1 teaspoon salt; blend until smooth. Set Instant Pot to SAUTÉ, and follow manufacturer's instructions to select middle temperature setting (NORMAL). Heat oil in metal insert until prompt indicates HOT. Add onion, celery, and carrots (roots only; set aside greens to use later); season generously with salt and pepper (about 1 teaspoon salt and ½ teaspoon pepper). Cook, stirring often, until vegetables have softened, about 10 minutes. Press CANCEL. Stir in wax and green beans, dried beans, bay leaf, thyme, reserved carrot tops, reserved tomato purée, and 6 cups (1½ quarts) water; season generously with salt (about 1 teaspoon). Close and lock the lid; seal valve (set to SEALING). Set to PRESSURE COOK with setting on HIGH. Set time to 35 minutes. When timer rings, press CANCEL; follow manufacturer's instructions to release pressure. Stir in broken noodles and squash. Return lid to pot and let stand until pasta and squash have softened, about 20 minutes. Season soup with additional salt to taste. Serve soup topped with a spoonful of pesto (or stir full amount in before serving). Remove bay leaf and thyme sprigs before serving.

Soup Club Pantry

The secret to a great soup is attention to detail, so consider this the cookbook equivalent of Caroline's little black book. Crafting your own spice blends rather than picking them up from the store means you can tweak the balance of flavors to your liking and make it truly your own.

These recipes mainly call for whole spices, which hold their flavor longer than ground versions and ensure a freshness you can't find in a store. These small-but-mighty recipes guarantee that "extra something" that will raise eyebrows and keep your friends and family coming back for seconds.

Homemade Curry Powder

Makes ½ cup

1 tablespoon cumin seed
2 teaspoons fenugreek seed
1 (4-inch) piece cinnamon stick, crushed into pieces
½ teaspoon black peppercorns
½ whole nutmeg, crushed into pieces
2 tablespoons turmeric
2 tablespoons ground ginger
2 teaspoons ground cardamom

1 / Heat a small, heavy skillet (such as cast-iron) over medium-high heat until hot; add cumin, fenugreek, cinnamon, peppercorns, and nutmeg. Toast spices until fragrant, crackling, and beginning to brown, about 2 minutes. Transfer toasted spices to a spice grinder and pulse until finely ground. Combine ground spices with turmeric, ginger, and cardamom. Transfer curry powder to an airtight container; store away from heat for up to 3 months.

Homemade Garam Masala

Makes ¼ cup

10 black peppercorns
10 whole cloves
10 cardamom pods, crushed slightly
1 teaspoon cumin seed
1 teaspoon coriander seeds
2 (4-inch) cinnamon sticks, crushed into pieces
½ whole nutmeg, crushed into pieces

1 / Heat a small, heavy skillet (such as cast-iron) over medium-high heat until hot; add peppercorns, cloves, cardamom, cumin, coriander, cinnamon, and nutmeg. Toast spices until fragrant, crackling, and beginning to brown, about 2 minutes. Transfer toasted spices to a spice grinder and pulse until finely ground. Transfer garam masala to an airtight container; store away from heat for up to 3 months.

Homemade Harissa

Makes ¾ cup

6 to 8 dried guajillo chiles (about 1½ ounces), or other favorite mild, dried chile
2 teaspoons whole coriander seeds
2 teaspoons whole cumin seeds
8 cloves garlic, peeled
Kosher salt
½ cup olive oil

1 / Pull stems off chiles; split chiles down the middle and scrape out seeds. Break, chop, and tear dried chiles into small pieces. (You should have about ¾ cup small chile pieces.)

2 / Heat a large, heavy skillet (such as cast-iron) over medium-high heat until hot. Add chiles, coriander, and cumin. Toast spices until fragrant, crackling, and beginning to brown, about 2 minutes. Transfer spices to a bowl. (Reserve skillet.)

3 / Raise heat under skillet to high until pan is very hot; add garlic. Cook, turning cloves occasionally, until garlic is charred in spots, about 5 minutes. Transfer reserved toasted spices to a blender jar with charred garlic, 1½ teaspoons salt, and ½ cup boiling water; blend until smooth. While the motor is running, drizzle in oil in a slow, steady stream. (The paste will become shiny and thick.) Transfer harissa paste to an airtight container; store in refrigerator for up to 2 weeks or freeze for up to 6 months.

Green Chili Powder

Makes ½ cup

2 tablespoons cumin seed
2 tablespoons coriander seed
2 dried bay leaves, broken into pieces
1 tablespoon dried oregano
2 tablespoons ground, dried mild Hatch chiles

1 / Heat a small, heavy skillet (such as cast-iron) over medium-high heat until hot; add cumin, coriander, and bay leaves. Toast spices until fragrant, crackling, and beginning to brown, about 2 minutes. Transfer toasted spices to a spice grinder with oregano and pulse until finely ground. Combine ground spices with ground chile. Transfer chili powder to an airtight container; store away from heat for up to 3 months.

Toasted Chili Powder

Makes ⅔ cup

6 to 8 dried guajillo chiles (about 1½ ounces) or other favorite mild chile
1 tablespoon coriander seed
1 tablespoon cumin seed
1 (1-inch) piece cinnamon stick, crushed into pieces
1 tablespoon dried oregano
1 tablespoon smoked paprika

1 / Pull stems off chiles; split chiles down the middle and scrape out seeds. Break, chop, and tear dried chiles into small pieces. (You should have about ¾ cup small chile pieces.)

2 / Heat a large, heavy skillet (such as cast-iron) over medium-high heat until hot; add chiles, coriander, cumin, and cinnamon. Toast spices until fragrant, crackling, and beginning to brown, about 2 minutes. Transfer toasted spices to a spice grinder with oregano and pulse until finely ground. Combine ground spices with paprika. Transfer chili powder to an airtight container; store away from heat for up to 3 months.

Vegan Nit'r Qibe

Makes 1½ cups

1 tablespoon black peppercorns
1 tablespoon cumin seeds
2 teaspoons fenugreek seeds
10 crushed cardamom pods
5 whole cloves
1 (3-inch) piece cinnamon stick, crushed
1 pound coconut oil (about 2 heaping cups)
1 small onion, sliced
4 cloves garlic, sliced
1 (2-inch) piece fresh ginger, sliced
2 teaspoons dried turmeric
1 tablespoon dried oregano

1 / Heat a medium saucepan over medium-high heat until hot; add peppercorns, cumin, fenugreek, cardamom, cloves, and cinnamon. Toast, stirring constantly, until spices are fragrant, crackling, and beginning to brown, about 2 minutes. Add oil, onion, garlic, ginger, turmeric, and oregano. Set pan over low heat. Cook, checking occasionally to make sure the onion doesn't sizzle, until oil is bright yellow and fragrant, about 30 minutes. Remove from heat; let stand, covered, until just warm to the touch, about 1 hour. Pour oil through a fine mesh sieve into a liquid measuring cup. (Compost solids.) Transfer strained nit'r qibe to an airtight container; store in refrigerator for up to 2 weeks or freeze for up to 6 months.

Berbere

Makes about ½ cup

2 teaspoons fenugreek seeds
2 Árbol chiles, crushed
8 whole cloves
12 whole cardamom pods, crushed
1 whole nutmeg, crushed
1 tablespoon garlic powder
1 tablespoon onion powder
1 tablespoon ground ginger
2 tablespoons paprika
1 teaspoon ground allspice

1 / Heat a small, heavy skillet (such as cast-iron) over medium-high heat until hot. Add fenugreek, chiles, cloves, cardamom, and nutmeg. Toast, stirring often, until spices are fragrant, crackling, and beginning to brown, about 2 minutes. Transfer spices to a spice grinder; blend until finely ground. Combine ground spices with garlic powder, onion powder, ginger, paprika, and allspice. Transfer berbere to an airtight container; store away from heat for up to 3 months.

Vegan Pesto

Makes 1 cup

3 packed cups basil leaves
3 cloves garlic, peeled, optional
¼ cup pumpkin seeds
¼ cup nutritional yeast
2 tablespoons freshly squeezed lemon juice
Kosher salt and freshly ground black pepper
¼ cup olive oil, plus more for storing

1 / Combine basil, garlic (if using), pumpkin seeds, nutritional yeast, lemon juice, 1½ teaspoons salt, and ½ teaspoon pepper with ¼ cup water in a blender jar; pulse to finely chop and form a sauce. In a slow, steady stream, drizzle in olive oil while pulsing motor. Transfer pesto to an airtight container; drizzle a thin layer of oil over top. Store pesto in refrigerator for up to 2 weeks or freeze for up to 6 months.

Homemade Cajun Seasoning

Makes ⅓ cup

6 to 8 dried guajillo chiles (about 1½ ounces) or other favorite mild, dried chile
1 tablespoon black peppercorns
2 teaspoons dried oregano
2 teaspoons dried thyme
1 tablespoon garlic powder
1 tablespoon onion powder

1 / Pull stems off chiles; split chiles down the middle and scrape out seeds. Break, chop, and tear dried chiles into small pieces. (You should have about ¾ cup small chile pieces.)

2 / Heat a large, heavy skillet (such as cast-iron) over medium-high heat until hot; add chiles and peppercorns. Toast spices until fragrant and beginning to brown, about 2 minutes. Transfer toasted spices to a spice grinder with oregano and thyme; pulse until finely ground. Combine ground spices with garlic and onion powders. Transfer seasoning to an airtight container; store away from heat for up to 3 months.

Homemade Grain-Free Flour Blend

Makes 4 cups

1 cup tapioca flour, spooned and leveled
1 cup arrowroot flour, spooned and leveled
1 cup coconut flour, spooned and leveled
1 cup almond flour, spooned and leveled

1 / Whisk together flours in a medium bowl. Transfer flour mixture to an airtight container; store away from heat for up to 3 months.

Bean Glossary

 Adzuki Beans: An ancient crop from eastern Asia that remains abundantly grown across the continent, adzuki beans are most well known for their confectionary use. Swap: small red beans.

 Black Beans: An ancient bean native to the Americas, black beans are a relative of the kidney bean and a staple for many cultures across Central and South America. Swap: pinto.

Black-Eyed Peas: The more well-known sibling of the cowpea, black-eyed peas are distinguished by their black spot and creamy texture when cooked; the countless heirloom varieties can feature an "eye" that is brown, red, pink, or green. Swap: navy.

Butter Beans: These flat, speckled beans are also known as "dwarf" or "baby limas"; they are less starchy than their mature form and are white when dried. Swap: Great Northern, navy.

 Cannellini Beans: Also known as "white kidney" for their similar shape and close relation, these beans are a staple in Italian cuisine thanks to Italian immigrants who brought them from Argentina. Swap: Great Northern, navy.

Chickpea: Also called garbanzos ("chana" in Indian supermarkets), chickpeas are round and firm and generally found in either a plump, large light tan variety, which are typical in American supermarkets, or a smaller, denser variety that can range in color from tan to dark brown or black. Ground chickpeas are used as a versatile, protein-rich alternative flour for gluten-free cooking and baking.

 Cranberry Beans: Also known as borlotti beans, cranberry beans have a creamy texture and are a staple in Italian cooking. Swap: pinto.

 Flageolet: A common bean originating in France, these small kidney-shaped beans are picked before maturity and dried to retain their green hue. Swap: mayacoba, navy.

 Great Northern Beans: These common beans were cultivated by original peoples in South America, then spread around the world through early trade routes. Swap: cannellini, navy.

 Kidney Beans: This common bean is a staple in a variety of cultures and is so called because of its resemblance in color and shape to a kidney. They can be toxic if undercooked.

 Lentils, Black: Black lentils, also known as Beluga or caviar lentils, are very small with a rich, earthy flavor. They retain their shape and texture when cooked. No need to soak before cooking.

Lentils, Brown: The most common in American supermarkets, brown lentils have a greenish tint. No need to soak before cooking.

Lentils, Green: The two main varieties hail from France (called either French or "Lentilles de Puy") and are prized for their firm texture in salads. They require the longest cooking time among lentil varieties.

Lentils, Red: These tiny orange, quick-cooking lentils are a very old crop thought to have originated in the Middle East or Mediterranean. No need to soak before cooking. Swap: yellow split peas.

Mayacoba Beans: Also called canario or, simply, Coba beans, this soft Peruvian bean is pale yellow and holds its shape well when cooked. Swap: cannellini, Great Northern.

Mung Bean: Alternatively spelled "moong," these nutrient-dense beans are used in both sweet and savory dishes by a variety of cultures. When sprouted, they are white and crunchy and are commonly sold in American grocery stores as "bean sprouts." When split in half, these beans are referred to as "moong dal." Swap: green lentils.

Navy Beans: Also called "small white beans," these common beans are a pale ivory color with a mild flavor. Swap: cannellini or Great Northern.

Pigeon Peas: Also known as Congo or Angola peas, these beans are popular in Asia, Africa, Latin America, and India with a wide range of uses. They need to be soaked and cooked longer than other beans to soften their crisp texture. Swap: black-eyed peas.

Pink Beans: Popular in Caribbean and Puerto Rican cuisine, these beans are small and dense. Swap: pinto, cranberry, small red beans.

Pinto Beans: "Frijol pinto" or the "painted bean" in Spanish, these beans are named for a pig breed with the same color and are found in traditional regional Mexican winter dishes from cold months when meat was unavailable. Swap: black beans, cranberry.

Small Red Beans: These plump, brick-red beans are a staple in New Orleans and widely used in the Caribbean. Swap: adzuki.

Split Peas: Whether green or yellow, "split pea" refers to peas that are dried, hulled, and split into their two natural halves. While either color have cultural preferences—green, a common English staple, and yellow, the choice for Indian daal recipes, for example—they are interchangeable. No need to soak before cooking. Swap: red lentils.

Yellow Eye: Possibly listed as "butterscotch Calypso" or "dot-eye" beans in recipes with roots in New England, these beans are reputed to be the original choice for Boston baked beans. Swap: navy, flageolet.

Index

My many thanks—

First and foremost, to my Seattle soup friends, the cooks who first made soup for me and I hoped to repay in kind. These soups belong to you, too.

To my Kickstarter soup community, thank you for making this book happen in the first place. Without you, these pages would still only live on a computer and in my mind.

To Alli, my agent and dear friend, I am grateful that our lives bring us together to enjoy only the most beautiful projects: our homes, our families, and our work. Thank you for being a next-level soup clubber.

To Jean, for all the excited Zoom meetings about soup, for believing in this book and the club behind it.

To Willow, my muse, whose talent rooted the very idea of this book. I am endlessly grateful to you and the world you create with only color and water.

To Josh, for your trust, deep kindness, and hunger for that next shot.

To Amy B, for stringing together only the most arresting, soulful words to describe your experience with my cooking.

To Amy C, my creative confidante, for meeting me over tea and bagels for nearly two years to talk about this project. You are the silent artist behind this whole book and made my dreams real from cover to cover.

To Sarah for being my first backer always.

To Michelle, my dear friend, for mailing me boxes of beans to continue my recipe testing and development when the entirety of Seattle bought all the lentils in fear of a virus.

To Kendra, whose creativity inspired mine in the form of a blueprint, for being a colleague.

To Robin, for being a keen tester and reader of my recipes. I couldn't have done this without your enthusiasm or willingness to be paid in soup.

To Carrie, my other intern extraordinaire, for your beautiful bean drawings. And for picking up boxes of produce on my front lawn and testing via video chat when a pandemic swept our city.

To Adam, for being my personal tech support and making modern what I can only seem to create in books.

To my dad, my most dedicated helper in all manner of things, without whom this project would have never happened. And to my mom, for the soup-related texts and a lifetime of quiet support.

To Garth, for being the dishwasher, resident taste tester, delivery driver, and my business manager. And for tolerating yet another wild idea that produces boxes of books stored in your office. To Henry, for eating soup for dinner and then finding it again in your lunchbox the next day with little complaint. To Theodore, for making gumbo with me on Valentine's Day and agreeing with your brother when he announces, "Mommy, you make the best soup!" This book, and all that I do, is for my three dinner companions. I love you endlessly.

About the Artists

Willow Heath, painter of soups

Willow Heath is a second-generation artist and first-time cookbook illustrator. She teaches illustration, watercolor, and portrait art at numerous Seattle schools, including Gage Academy of Art and Pratt Fine Arts Center. She and Caroline worked together on Caroline's picture book, *Lasting Love*. Her favorite soups to paint are those she loves to eat, like the Moroccan Vegetable Stew (page 19) she painted for the cover of this book.

Instagram @willowheath / willowheath.com

Joshua Huston, photographer

Joshua Huston is a commercial and editorial photographer who loves making authentic images that inspire an emotional connection with viewers. When he isn't creating editorial work for magazines, he conceives visual marketing and branding content for companies. Joshua is also Caroline's neighbor and a soup club member. He vehemently insists that Teddy's Black Bean Soup (page 13) is the best he's ever had in his life.

Instagram @joshuahustonphoto / joshuahuston.com

Amy Baranski, soup haiku poet

Amy Baranski is a haiku poet and high-tech professional. She has been published in *Acorn* magazine and in the *New Bridges* and *Seabeck* haiku anthologies. When she's not at her desk eating soup, thinking about Caroline's Pumpkin-Coconut Soup with Curry Leaves (page 9), or writing soup-inspired haiku, you might find her on the trails in the Pacific Northwest having a moss moment, soup mug in hand. Amy learned haiku from Johnny Baranski, her late father and renowned haiku poet of North America. Literary haiku, the kind Amy practices, typically shuns the 5-7-5 form. It prioritizes sharing a poignant moment, as the poet experiences, in three short lines, with a seasonal reference.

Twitter @amybaranski

About the Book

This book was first created and published by me, Caroline, the author. (Hi.) I wanted to bind in book form the feeling that my soups seemed to pass along to my friends, how it feels to be a member of soup club. From a tender place in my heart I began making these soups for friends who, in turn, honored them by building rituals around them and brought them into their homes to feed the ones they love the most. When I was invited into their homes with a photographer for this book, I was able to live their rituals with them and help tell that story. I knew I didn't want photos of *soup* in the book—largely because I don't think the qualities of soup, what it offers to the person who makes and shares it, are best represented in realistic means. Soup is a mood, a feeling, a moment. That's why I asked my friend Willow to paint the soups in watercolor and my friend Amy to write the haiku. Their perspectives translated and represented what I could not. They agreed and traded their art for soup, which felt like a soulful exchange of the highest sort.

And so the book came to life. It found its own vibrant community of grateful and excited soup lovers who reacted viscerally to it, diving immediately into its pages to develop soup rituals of their own, connected by these pages despite finding them amidst the isolation of the coronavirus pandemic. It occurs to me now that the book is all I wanted for it and more: it, like the club and even the soups themselves, seems to communicate joy and bring people together.

That you—yes, you, holding this book—have it in your hands means you now perhaps see soup the way my friends and I do. Since there isn't a secret handshake or anything, I'll do the next best thing: to simply welcome you to the club. I hope you'll share this book with your favorite people, offered with a uniquely personal comfort to each person who holds it, like only the very best soup can.

Caroline

Caroline's recipes and articles appear regularly online and in national lifestyle publications, including *Bon Appétit*, *Food and Wine*, *Food Network*, *Every Day with Rachael Ray*, *The Kitchn*, and *Food52*. Wright is the author of four cookbooks that range from cakes to Catalan cuisine, though her passion for community and storytelling is woven throughout each book. Her terminal brain cancer diagnosis in 2017 shifted her focus from career to health and family and she began authoring children's books for her two sons. She lives in Seattle, Washington, where she is lovingly known as the soup lady.